Growing On Purpose

The Formula to Strengthen Your Team

AND Improve Your Customer Experience

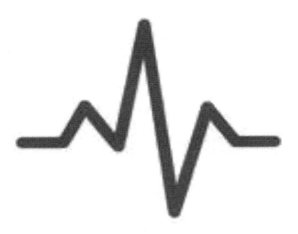

A Positive Polarity Book

By Dave Molenda *with* Reji Laberje

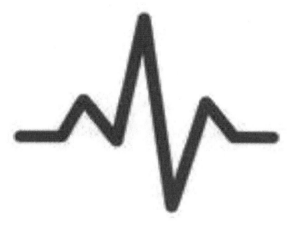

<u>What Others Say . . .</u>

"I wish I would have had Dave's *book "Growing on Purpose - The Formula to Strengthen Your Team AND Improve Your Customer Experience" when I was trying to grow the businesses that I have managed or started. The specifics of his game plan and the priority he gives the customer experience in that plan may just change the way you think about growth...for the good."*

~Wayne Breitbarth
Author of the Power Formula for LinkedIn Success:
Kick-start, Your Business, Brand and Job Search

"Exceptional sales professionals are among the toughest roles to hire and retain because of their seemingly innate ability to ferret out opportunities, build relationships, and close deals. But exceptional sales professionals can be taught and developed under the right coach. I would hire Dave in a second to coach my sales team and speak at a sales event or conference. He combines an impressive sales pedigree and entrepreneurial background with his expertise in strength-based selling and DISC assessments to help underperforming sales teams amp up their game and top performers reach even greater heights. He's personable, funny, and can engage any team. I love his premise of getting to the heart of prospect and client

needs to establish trust and tell a compelling story. I also think his practical, boots on ground focus on the importance of sales analytics, metrics, goals, and activities to build pipeline is integral to any company's success. "

~Jessica Akin
Author and President of Trust the Journey

"Dave Molenda displays the best of positive, passionate business skills. His keen sense of process, combined with a firm grasp of the challenges business face, provides solid insight for leaders today. Dave is a solid, forward-thinking, servant leader!"

Nick Ringger
The Community Warehouse

"They say 'A rising tide; lifts all ships' Dave Molenda and his message of positivity and connection serves as that tide wherever he goes, sharing his experience and best practices. I am speaking from personal experience both as a client of his professional coaching and having hired him as speaker at my professional organization's annual meeting (300+ people). He won over the audience of the two sessions he lead working with business owners

on Communications and Employee Engagement and got invited back to speak at the following years meeting by the Board before he left."

Cheryl L. Gendron
Director of Communications and Events

"Dave has been a part of our team for many years. Dave brings his knowledge and enthusiasm to every meeting. He continues to stimulate and educate our team understanding of who we are and how we can best relate. Dave offers a professional yet spirited approach to building positive team relationships. We can count on him to teach us new and important life lessons at each meeting we have. We enjoy working with Dave and continue to place our confidence in him and the way he helps our team interact with each other and all those we meet!"

Richard Scherer
Owner, Deep River Partners

"Dave shares his unique take on leadership through stories of persevering in the construction industry during the 2008 economic downturn. Tried and true leadership approaches coupled with real examples of leadership success makes this a relevant read for any leader."

Jennifer Buchholz
Bestselling Author and Owner of Transform Via Travel

This work is based on the experiences of an individual. Every effort has been made to ensure the accuracy of the content.

Quantity order requests can be emailed to: **publishing@rejilaberje.com**
Or mailed to:
Reji Laberje Author Programs
Publishing Orders
234 W. Broadway Street
Waukesha, WI 53186

Molenda, Dave
Growing On Purpose; How to Strengthen Your Team and Improve Your Customer's Experience
Contributing Author: Reji Laberje, Reji Laberje Writing and Publishing
Contributing Editor: RaeAnne Scargall
Interior Design: Reji Laberje
Cover Design: Michael Nicloy
Photos and Graphics: Dave Molenda, Kimberly Laberge

ISBN-10 1945907029
SBN-13: 978-1945907029

Categories:
Business & Money/Business Culture/Health & Stress
Business & Money/Human Resources/Conflict Resolution & Mediation
Business & Money/Management & Leadership/Training

BISAC Codes:
BUS110000 BUSINESS & ECONOMICS / Conflict Resolution & Mediation
BUS041000 BUSINESS & ECONOMICS / Management
BUS106000 BUSINESS & ECONOMICS / Mentoring & Coaching

Writing and Publishing
www.rejilaberje.com

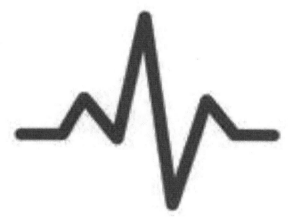

<u>Dedication</u>

According to Gallup's Study on "The State of the Global Workplace", 29% of our workforce is engaged in their job, 53% of our workforce is not engaged and 18% is actively disengaged.

ENGAGED PEOPLE are psychologically committed to their jobs, while making positive contributions to the organization. NOT ENGAGED PEOPLE lack the motivation and are less likely to invest discretionary effort in organizational goals or outcomes. ACTIVELY DISENGAGED PEOPLE are unhappy, unproductive and liable to spread negativity to co-workers.

***This book is dedicated to all three of these groups.** If you are not part of the 29% of engaged people, my hope is that this will stir up something within you to make a difference: start with a new attitude, a new course; find the motivation and be the absolute best team member that you can be; look inwardly first, before you point at others' faults. YOU CAN GROW ON PURPOSE!*

If you are part of the 29%, this is dedicated to you, as well. It is my hope that you can continue to fight the good fight and maybe even bring some of the less engaged with you as you head to a better place, a place where you all can GROW ON PURPOSE!

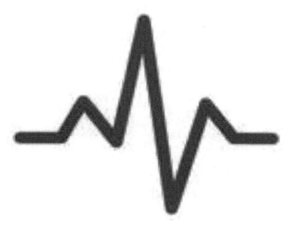

<u>Forward</u>

About this Book

According to the U.S. Bureau of Labor Statistics, Wisconsin ranked 44th out of 50 states for job growth in the year 2004 – its worst year in the history of its statehood.

In 1986, at age twenty-one, I had my first job as an outside sales person. I had been hired as a manufacturer's representative to sell a specific product. Calls came in from architects, to commercial builders, to retailers. It's funny how you remember the dates of firsts in your life. For me, this first was on May nineteenth and the workday began at 8:00 A.M. My first call came in at 8:10 A.M. and, by 9:00 A.M.; I was sitting in front of the prospect at an off-site meeting. I didn't know ANYTHING. There had to be a better way. Still, as with most young adults, I fiddled around until I figured it out and ultimately learned to excel.

By 1991, I was in a sales management position working in my company's new (and unfunded) division focused on selling construction products. It was the start of a growing mini-empire and for many years, through hard work, the division became successful and profitable. It wasn't until seventeen years later, in 2008, that I ever had to look at doing business differently. Since then, I have come to realize the importance of reinventing yourself regularly.

It's no surprise to anybody who was an adult at that time that 2008 was the year that was all about the economy. Building permits dropped significantly. For the construction industry, it was another blow in the middle of a long downturn. In 2004, in Wisconsin, Building permits dropped every year from 40,178 given in a year, down to the 2011 bottom of 9,968. On the ride down to this seventy-five percent drop, we had a wakeup call. We could either close the doors or figure out a way, against the odds, to stay in business. We decided to grow our business . . . intentionally.

We built through education. Our education wasn't aimed at informing people about our product. What we were building was relationships and strong clients. My thought was, *'if our customers were kept in business, we'd still stay in business, too.'* We taught them the tools they needed to use to keep going strong: LinkedIn training, QuickBooks workshops, sales and marketing training, and even memory training to help our clients with personal and inter-relational growth. Our job became all about helping them to keep their jobs. We put ourselves in the customers' shoes and thought, *'what would we want from our vendor or valued partner?'*

Then, we engaged our team. We went to full transparency with them so that they understood the importance of our new brand of customer service. With transparency came trust.

At a time when we should have been in survivor mode, we ended up in thriver mode. We grew our market share fifty-seven percent and, in 2013, this company—that had begun as an unfunded division of just one (ME!)—now boasted a twenty-two person team with sales of just under ten million dollars. We did it by focusing on both our internal team members, and our external customers.

Internal team members ARE customers, also. We need to serve one another. It's important to approach our own teams in the same positive tones and methods as we use for our clients. Throughout this book, you may hear me refer to the internal customer, and that means the team.

I learned to love the trainings that my company held. I enjoyed helping others succeed. I enjoyed watching our clients learn new things and seeing the light bulbs come on when business owners found answers to help them through difficult times and they expressed gratitude when we helped them with intentional growth. From my vantage point, I could then witness owners and managers as they taught their teams and realized that it was the trainings that they were receiving—somewhat of an anomaly in the construction world—that were really making a positive, profitable difference in their companies. More than one client expressed that we helped them stay in business with our education and outside-of-the-box thinking.

From a relatively comfortable place, I had a choice to make. I could fly under the radar for another ten years, or take the momentum I'd built up in trainings—a newfound passion for coaching—to a full-time job! It was almost like having a woodshop where you made a single shelf that somebody needed. On the one hand, you're happy that you made a difference to that one person, but on the other hand, you realize that you now know how to make these shelves and you're able to recognize two things at one time: 1) you want to put that shelf into more hands, and 2) doing so will be hard work.

After twenty-eight years, I told my business partner that I was leaving to start *Positive Polarity*. To do so, I tapped back into my outside sales roots and grew my client base. I knew people and grew businesses and helped them. I got into speaking wherever I could. I went to business owners to whom I knew I could bring value. Almost every time I speak locally, I gain a customer out of it.

Because of my value for continual training and development to grow professionally, I became a Certified Professional Behavior Analyst (CPBA), a Certified Professional Motivator's Analyst (CPMA), and DISC-Certified. If you're not moving forward, you may as well be moving backwards. Customers want to work with companies moving in the same direction as them.

I've seen the inside team experience and the outside customer experience, but they were usually viewed as two silos, with few connections. Some places are starting to recognize the need to marry the two business houses, but it's happening primarily in those companies with high budgets or rocketing capital, as with Google and Zappos. What about the small and medium businesses that want to make the necessary changes to not run by default, but rather to have profitability on purpose?

That's who this book is for. It's for those who need to grow on purpose, with purpose, and through purposeful steps.

When deciding on a logo to represent my company, Positive Polarity, I wanted something that reflected action and purpose together. The heartbeat monitor came to represent, not only those things, but also that "heart check" that every business and leader must have. Throughout this book, you'll have opportunities to take a beat – a moment – to reflect on powerful, positive messages. These are our "Upbeats" and

UPbeat!

Find and record your own Upbeats throughout "Growing on Purpose"!

you'll have an opportunity to read some of mine and also create some of your own.

"Growing On Purpose" is a Reji Laberje Writing and Publishing interactive text. In this book, you will find QR codes that will provide insight into what is being shared. Find a free QR scanner for your smart device via a search through your device's app store. Scan the inserted QR codes with your smart device to discover online resources. Further information from the QR codes can be found on the Electronic Resource Hub (ERH) for *"Growing On Purpose"* and on the Positive Polarity website.

Want to try it out? Visit the ERH through the below QR code.

Electronic Resource Hub
"Growing On Purpose"
www.rejilaberje.com/dave-molenda.html

And check out my company page:
Positive Polarity
http://positivepolarity.com/

Get ready to strengthen your team and improve your customers' experience to create profit.

Are you ready to see your business growth manifested?

Table of Contents

Introduction

PART 1 – Strengthen Your Team

Two Questions

A - Acknowledge Thyself

B - A Sense of Belonging

    Trust

    Compassion

    Stability

    Hope

C - Migrating to the Communication Comfort Zone

PART 2 – Improve Your Customer Experience

The External D's – Your Customer's Experience

    Decide

    Determine

    Design

    Deliver

    Dare to Differ

E is for Engagement

    Survival

    Security

    Belonging

    Importance

    Self-Actualization

PART 3 – The Profit Will Come

Guidance and Support

Resources

Acknowledgments

About the Authors

po·lar·i·ty (noun):

The presence or manifestation of two opposite or contrasting principles or tendencies.

<u>Introduction</u>

On the Way to Work

According to Forbes, 19% of Americans arrive late to work at least once a week.

An interesting scene takes place at the elevator each morning as the team heads in to work for the day. How many of you can relate to the chaos and stress of this "indoor commuting" experience?

Dylan is running behind (and a bit agitated as a result).

At last, the door opens, and Dylan is the first one on.

Immediately, Dylan presses the floor of choice . . . multiple times, even while others start to file in.

Indi gets on and completely ignores the floor buttons when noticing another person on the elevator.

Indi completely engages in conversation with this person.

Dylan proceeds to move from pushing the numbered floor button to pushing the <CLOSE DOOR> button.

No matter; Sam holds the elevator door open, allowing Chris to go ahead onto the elevator.

Sam peeks in to see if there is still room for one more.

Chris immediately locates the elevator's "capacity plate" and starts counting the people.

Sam barely makes it on before noticing Chris giving a sideways glance to a heavier person on the back of the elevator.

Dylan is still clicking the <CLOSE DOOR> button.

At the last second, Sam hops off to accommodate nervous-looking Chris.

Indi finishes the first elevator conversation and attempts to engage Dylan, but gets a one-word response and nothing more.

The leader waits for the elevator doors to open several floors up; when they open . . .

Dylan is upset that a simple elevator ride took so long.

Indi is upset because Dylan wouldn't engage in conversation.

Chris is uncomfortable and eager to get out of the cramped space.

Sam arrives late and out of breath, from the stairs, with a cup of coffee for the leader.

The leader, feeling a bit agitated, today, only connects briefly with Dylan before it's time for them all to start their day.

- What if Dylan, Indi, Sam, and Chris were the four people on your team?
- What do you know about them?
- How do you work with them?
- How could you get each of them to enter their work days positively?
- If you don't get your team working together positively, as a strong unit, what kind of customer experience do you think they'll provide?
- If you don't provide a quality customer experience, how do you expect to have a fully engaged business?
- Without a fully engaged business, how will the business be profitable?

And what if some simple ABC's could make that daily elevator exit, the work day, the customer experience, your business's engagement level, and your profit all positive despite the existing professional polarities in your staff?

There is a model that can be achieved when leaders ask these questions of themselves and take the necessary steps to intentional improvement:

Before continuing into the work of ***"Growing On Purpose,"*** take a moment to reflect on the elevator scene.

1. To which character do you most relate and why?

2. Which character do you think would be the most difficult to relate to and why?

3. Do you think the relationships in your professional life effect the work you produce and why?

Seek first to understand
and then be understood.
~Stephen Covey

Part 1:

Strengthening Your Team

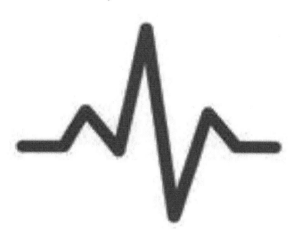

<u>Two Questions</u>

Improve the Elevator Experience

According to Stephanie Rising, 10% of people are Dominant, 25% of people are Influencers, 40% of people are Steady, and 25% of people are Compliant.

Some of the first things I researched and learned, when training and coaching became my career IPath, were behaviors and motivators. While there are a number of popular strength assessments, personality profile tests, type indicators, and attitude identifiers, I chose to use DISC. DISC has become popular in the professional world, particularly in the last twenty or so years, but the DISC personality assessment was originally created by PhD. William Moulton Marston in 1928. It's been modified and improved upon by professionals and psychologists in the almost century of implementation since, but it is as respected and—some would say—even more accurate than other assessments such as Myers-Briggs. The latter was actually not originally published until four years after the initial DISC emotional profiles.

I was driven to learn about the process of profiling for personality types because of the poor communication I had been a part of or witnessed throughout my career. I recognized that there was a potential for harmful disconnects and miscommunications between persons. A lot of that disconnect comes down to what type of personalities the people in the conversation have.

Every successful sitcom of the past half a century makes sure to have representatives of the four DISC personality types: Dominance, Influence, Steady, and Compliance. From *"I Love Lucy,"* to *"M*A*S*H,"* to *"Cheers,"* to *"FRIENDS,"* each program has had a person in the cast to whom the audience members in the general population could relate. Why? Because the audience was so vast and they were unsure who was watching. In the era of Nielsen ratings, producers wanted to be certain television viewers would connect with somebody.

When I became certified in DISC, I discovered that one's personality type is a big part of determining *at least* that person's:

- Motivation
- Priorities
- What an Individual Trusts
- What Bothers an Individual

Looking back at the morning elevator scenario, imagine a leader who was aware of his staffs' personalities and helped them to be aware of one another's personalities as well. Imagine that the team had communicated about the differences they had in motivation and priorities. Imagine that they understood the things that could turn off or shut down their colleagues.

Everybody would recognize that Dylan is Dominant. As a "D," Dylan is results-oriented and time bound; Dylan trusts confidence and is bothered by small talk; Dylan dismisses the little details and dislikes when a presumed authority is challenged. We would know that Indi, who has the "Influence" personality, prefers action, enthusiasm and relationships. Sam trusts openness and is bothered by what could be perceived as negative callousness. Steady Sam is seeking to accommodate others while Chris needs to address very specific and measurable objectives.

If these four people, and the leader who awaits them on their work floor, simply recognize their differences, how could the day get off to a better start?

Dylan is still the first on the elevator, but instead of pushing the <CLOSE DOOR> button, the <OPEN DOOR> button is pushed. Dylan is still in control; so as long as it's Dylan's finger on the button, the Dominant personality is not offended. Dylan makes eye contact with Indi so that Indi doesn't feel ignored, but it is Sam for whom Indi waits. Sam engages Indi due to the accommodating nature of a Steady personality. Sam even confirms to Chris that the capacity of the elevator is fine.

When the doors open on the work floor, the leader says "good morning," to Dylan first, and then lets Dylan go. The leader doesn't want to get the Dominant personality off-track, short of some big picture initiatives for the day. With Indi, the leader may ask how the family is doing. "Can I help you with anything today?" could be a common approach to Indi each day before asking when a report or other to-do item will be ready. Sam needs to pull out a calendar and also seeks input and opportunities to accommodate the leader while Chris is given some specific detail-oriented objectives to accomplish.

The difference between a negative and positive start to this team's work day (and ultimately their overall engagement, the customer experience, and the bottom line) is simply knowing how to read one another and respond appropriately. A successful organization (just like those successful sitcoms) are likely to have a mix of team members who are dominant, influencing, steady, and compliant, and this is a good and healthy reality. A leader may initially look for dominance in the people put in charge as these are often the innovators, but organizations are just as much in need of relationship makers typically found among influencers, customer service persons who often have steady personalities and accounting, engineering, or human resources people that are common among compliant personalities. This is not to say that these particular areas are the only roles for the related personality types; it is more likely that there may exist some natural draws to certain types of work among the dominant, influencing, steady, and compliant personalities. Furthermore, *all* types are needed in a professional engine and everybody will do their best work when communicated with according to type.

Assessments are a great way to learn about a team and its leadership. If you have the resources to bring in a certified assessor, it could be a great exercise in building a team as a unit, but it

UPbeat!

The difference between a negative and a positive start to a team's work day (and ultimately its overall engagement, the customer experience, and the bottom line) is simply knowing how to respond appropriately.

doesn't have to be so complicated. For the purposes of working through team strengthening and improving the customer experience, let's break down the in-depth assessment process to a simple two-question survey.

1. **Are you more of an impulsive person (fast) or more of a calculated person (methodical)?**

2. **Do you communicate and base decisions more on relationships (people) or on data (facts)?**

While *"Growing On Purpose"* does not focus specifically on DISC personalities, for simplicity, consider what these two questions could identify for you, as a leader:

Personality	Fast	Methodical	People	Facts
Dominance	Yes	No	No	Yes
Influence	Yes	No	Yes	No
Steady	No	Yes	Yes	No
Compliance	No	Yes	No	Yes

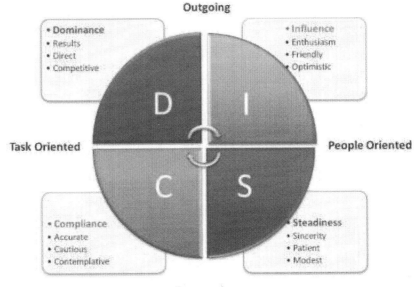

With just two questions, leaders have a starting point as to how to communicate with their teams.

With just two questions, leaders can help to identify team strengths.

With just two questions, leaders can help a team engage in the customer . . . and company . . . *experience*.

With just two questions, a company can begin the fundamental steps toward profit.

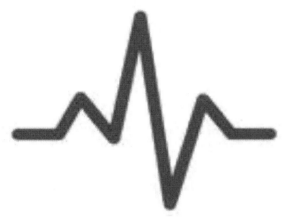

"Employees who believe that management is concerned about them as a whole person – not just an employee – are more productive, more satisfied, more fulfilled. Satisfied employees mean satisfied customers, which leads to profitability."
~Anne M. Mulcahey

Acknowledge Thyself

Start with a Blank Page

According to a 2010 study of seventy-two senior executives from thirty-one different companies by Green Peak Partners and Cornell's School of Industrial Labor and Relations, self-aware leaders with strong, interpersonal skills deliver better financial performance.

E arly in my leadership years, I noticed that, if I were in front of a group of twenty people in my company, speaking in the way I would like to be spoken to in return, some of the people would stay with me . . . *some of them.* It didn't matter whether the topic was sales training, leadership, or specific to a project; I started to notice that a group of people weren't staying with me. It wasn't that they didn't understand what I was saying. Some people seemed disengaged simply because the flow of the meeting didn't work for them.

I could actually see people internalize and process differently. I would answer the questions of those who wanted clarification and see others methodically take their time to work through scenarios. In reality, these methodical processors weren't disengaged; they just needed a little more time.

It would be easy, as a leader, to discard those who don't react in the way that we might choose to respond in the same situation.

On the customer side, particularly in sales situations, it would also be easy to get frustrated. A fast-paced personality type may be seeking a signature when a more calculated person might want to Read.Every.Single.Word. (And then require a detail-oriented third party opinion of the paperwork.)

It got even worse when realizing that not everybody learned in the visual way that I learned. Some wanted to hear the message, while others were better with hands-on learning. People learn one of three ways. They learn visually, by seeing; they learn auditory, by hearing; or, they learn kinesthetically, by actually doing. Sixty-five percent of the population learns by seeing. A smaller percentage of people (about twenty-eight percent) learn by hearing and only about seven percent of people learn by touch, or doing.

It's very important that you understand how your clients learn and how your team learns so that you know how to share a message with them in such a way that it will resonate with them. If you're a visual person and I tell you ten things to do in an auditory way, the likelihood of you grasping all that is slim to none. When you understand how your clients and team learn, you're able to mimic that learning style. An email is good for somebody visual, as it's laid out for that person in print. An auditory learner would benefit from a follow-up phone call. A doer, or kinesthetic learner, may need you to walk through step-by-step with him or her. Consider in which of the three ways you most prefer your learning: visual, auditory, or kinesthetic. To take it to the next step, it's important to also ask yourself whether your client (or team member) learns in the same way.

Within my team, my partners, and with my customer base, I noticed the disparity between reactions to me from roughly half of the people I spoke to.

By taking a personality assessment, I learned about my own personality type and learning style. It was important for me to understand that I was dominant and visual, not to determine that this was a "right" way of communicating and learning, but because the first part of understanding others is understanding yourself. You must know what it is you bring to the table in order to find understanding in others.

If you don't know yourself, it would be easy to start an interaction that is self-focused, not necessarily on purpose, but with an agenda based on your own communication style. Fast-paced people dominate, methodical personality types allow the domination, and nobody leaves the conversation feeling fulfilled.

In Stephen Covey's respected book, *"7 Habits of Highly Successful People,"* he addresses the need for understanding in his fifth habit:

UPbeat!

The first part of understanding others is understanding yourself.

HABIT 5: SEEK FIRST TO UNDERSTAND, THEN TO BE UNDERSTOOD

Communication is the most important skill in life. You spend years learning how to read and write, and years learning how to speak. But what about listening? What training have you had that enables you to listen so you really, deeply understand another human being? Probably none, right?

If you're like most people, you probably seek first to be understood; you want to get your point across. And in doing so, you may ignore the other person completely, pretend that you're listening, selectively hear only certain parts of the conversation or attentively focus on only the words being said, but miss the meaning entirely. So why does this happen? Because most people listen with the intent to reply, not to understand. You listen to yourself as you prepare in your mind what you are going to say, the questions you are going to ask, etc. You filter everything you hear through your life experiences, your frame of reference. You check what you hear against your autobiography and see how it measures up. And consequently, you decide prematurely what the other person means before he/she finishes communicating.

So, why begin with yourself if your goal is to understand others?

We don't have control over how others are going to react in a communication or situation, only over how we are going to react in situations and communications. By understanding yourself, you can choose to use that knowledge to adjust your own communication style and teaching or learning approach in order to understand others. In other words, "seek first to understand and then be understood."

I used my knowledge of myself to discover the areas for improvement that existed in my own person. As a dominant personality, I needed to keep my controlling side in check and make certain that I didn't take over in a conversation. However, because I didn't want to lose my own engagement in communications, I had to find a way that I could be involved when not sharing my own ideas. I needed to work on being PRESENT in conversations in which I was the listener. This is an intentional choice and practice.

For me, the purposeful action I took to ensure that I was both engaged and listening, was to take, not *my* ideas or notes along, but a blank notepad in order to write down the thoughts of others.

1. Based on the two-question survey as well as with consideration to your learning style, what do you understand about yourself and how you behave in conversations?

2. Are there purposeful actions you need to take to ensure that you are engaged to understand rather than seeking to be understood in conversations?

If your emotional abilities aren't in hand, if you don't have self-awareness, if you are not able to manage your distressing emotions, if you can't have empathy and have effective relationships, then no matter how smart you are, you are not going to get very far.
~Daniel Goleman

A Sense of Belonging

Trust, Stability, Compassion, and Hope

According to a formal Gallup Group study conducted on over 10,000 individuals between 2005 and 2008, we have a very clear picture of what we need from the leaders who have influence in our lives

The hardest part of my early sales career for me was coming to terms with the word, "persuade." I felt like that term was negative. I thought "persuasion" made me seem like I was convincing people *away* from a current vendor, or away from an existing manner of doing business. I wasn't trying to steal from somebody else's camp. It seemed slimy or dishonest.

What I really wanted was to have others discover on their own *why* to do something. Then, I wanted to help provide solutions. I realized that my approach was to try to influence others through relationships. For me, motivation needed to be outward looking (focusing on the client relationship) and I needed to feel that I was a part of designing the sales process. I needed to know for myself what behaviors I have and what motivates me.

In a team setting, the details were everything. I needed to recognize the details and steps that my team members were making in order to be able to give necessary kudos for jobs well done. . If leaders don't acknowledge the details, there's a risk that teams will feel unimportant.

After a lifetime of professional experiences, I had the benefit of three very different perspectives with regard to the team environment. I'd experienced business to client relationships. I'd been a leader. I'd worked on a team. From these three perspectives, there was one thing that was common. We all desire a sense of belonging to our work if we're going to be truly engaged in that work.

What Gallup recognized in its study is that belonging, for a team member, is directly related to how influential they feel their leader is.

When asking:

1. "What leader has the most positive influence in your daily life?" and
2. "Now, list words that best describe what this person contributes to your life,"

Gallup discovered that what we most want, and what most contributes to that sense of belonging are: trust, stability, compassion, and hope. These are some shared ideas about what is expected professionally to contribute to these four areas.

Trust

To generate trust, teams need to feel:

- They are "in the know" about the company's big picture
- They understanding the future vision and trajectory of the company
- They understand their roles in the vision

Stability

To generate a feeling of stability the team needs to be confident in:
- A personal financial future
- The company's financial future
- The strength of the leadership

Compassion

The feeling of compassion can be expressed by:
- Putting people in front of profits
- Having empathy for the team
- Sharing in philanthropic efforts together as a team

Hope

To instill hope, teams need to experience in the workplace:
- A safe environment
- Both routine and unexpected encouragement
- Striving for "better" while experiencing contentment

Knowing what it is that a team needs to create a sense of belonging and achieving it are two different things. Let's look at each of the words and how to make them come to life in your business.

UPbeat!

Knowing what a team needs to create a sense of belonging and achieving it are two different things.

Trust

Studies have found that our perceptions of how much other people trust us are much higher than actual trust levels. In other words, we tend to overestimate, sometimes significantly, the level of trust others have in us. A Gallup poll revealed that the chances of team members being engaged at work if they do not trust the company leaders are just one in twelve. The same poll found that, with trust, chances increase to one in two!

UPbeat!

The chances of team members being engaged at work if they do not trust the company leaders are just one in twelve.

In regards to trust, Gallup's research shows that ninety-six percent of engaged employees trust their leadership and, of those employees who are considered disengaged, just forty-six percent trust their leadership. As the adage goes, "Which came first? The chicken (distrust) or the egg (disengagement)?

Distrust is a self-perpetuating cycle that has the power to grind an organization down to a crippling pace . . . or even to a halt.

Let's look at some of the discoveries made regarding some of the other effects trust (or distrust) can have on a company:

- 39% of individuals say they would start business or increase business with a company based solely on trust
- 53% of individuals say they would stop, reduce, or switch business to a competitor because of concerns about a company's trust
- 83% of individuals say they are more likely to "give the benefit of the doubt" to a company they trust and listen to them about without judgment in a difficult situation

- 64% of leaders say they have refused to buy a product or service of a company they did not trust

"Trust is more than a bonus. It is a tangible asset that must be created, sustained, and built upon . . . just as trust benefits companies, mistrust or lost trust has costs."
~Annual Edelman Trust Barometer

If you have ever started a new business relationship with a manufacturer or vendor, you know the drill. At first, you both meet to do your best to "sell" yourself to the other person. It looks like a dance of peacocks showing off their feathers to see who is the best, brightest, and most connected.

If you actually listen to the conversation between the manufacturer and distributor, you'll notice that they tend to miss some key points that would make the relationship more effective. Often, the two parties are working individually rather than toward a partnership. "Partnership" is a word that is used in many companies today. Before you say to yourself, 'I am covered there; we really partner with our distributor or manufacturer,' Look closely at the definition of "partnership":

Partnership is defined as a contractual relationship between two or more persons carrying on a joint business venture with a view to profit, *each incurring liability for losses* and the right to share in the profits. It sounds harmless enough, but what happens when you specifically focus on the second part of the definition? ". . . each incurring liability for losses."**

Wait a minute. I'm supposed to be responsible for the losses of my partner, and not just their gains? That is what the definition says. If you are not open to loss, then it might be best to refrain from using the term.

Partnership requires trust and trust is one of the things that studies find is most lacking in many business relationships today.

Working with someone means taking risks. If the partnership lacks trust, one partner is left constantly second guessing the other, which makes the team highly ineffective and ultimately unsuccessful.

Here's something to consider if you think that you are immune from low trust:

A recent survey of 750 manufacturers and 500 distributors revealed that eighty-two percent of manufacturers and ninety-two percent of distributors believe that sales performance and profitability are being negatively impacted by problems in the working relationship that they have – in other words, poor working relationships. It's safe to say many people blame competition, the economy, or even the government for their sales problems. These statistics point to something completely different; US!

Manufacturers said that the biggest problem with distribution is the lack of commitment to the products and promotional programs that the manufacturers offered. They also said that the distributors lack sales and marketing skills.

Distributors say that the primary problem with trust is inconsistent management of territories by the manufacturer. There are multiple and often conflicting channels to market, including direct selling. Only seventeen percent of distributors indicated that they have clearly-defined plans with manufacturers for accomplishing their sales goals. In addition, forty-nine percent of manufacturers and forty-two percent of distributors said that the overall level of commitment in their working relationships is very low.

The best part about trust is that there are many things within your grasp that you can do to build the necessary element in your relationships with your "partners." Scan the code to read about trust strategies on my blog at: http://positivepolarity.com/they-dont-trust-you-for-the-same-reason-you-dont-trust-them/

With the team, what erodes trust?

In a company, a lot of trust is built from the first job interview. Trust can break down if the conversation doesn't feel open or if there are inconsistencies between the person's resume and references and the experiences learned about through the on-boarding process. From the team side, trust can break down if existing staff aren't a part of the hiring process at all. Do they know what positions are being filled? Does leadership ask for their input?

It may be on the leadership to build a team with trustworthy members, but then it is on the team to maintain that trust. Trust can break down: if there isn't follow-through on assigned or promised tasks, if time and time management are not respected, and if there isn't an intentional effort by team members to work in harmony.

With the team, what builds trust?

Contrarily, a trust-builder is to have honesty and openness from the very beginning, starting with accuracy during the interview process. Imagine a scenario when a potential employee left his or her last employer on a sour note. There are diplomatic and respectful ways to express that reality to an interviewer, rather than waiting for him or her to find out when calling the past employer. Being open from the start would be less damaging than giving glowing recollections of a past job only to have the interviewer feel like he or she has been lied to.

Once a part of the team, the team needs to have follow-through, open communication, and reliability to build trust.

Trust creates buy-in . . . and a sense of belonging!

How can a leader erode trust?

A leader can erodes trust through instability. This shows up in a lack of contingencies and long-term goals. If a leader is too dialed into the present, how does the team know about the future? These leaders are seen as running a reactionary business rather than an action-oriented one.

Trust can also be eroded *to* the leader (and, by observation, to the team) if there is not a clear ability to share the load. If a leader constantly reaches out to pass a baton and there isn't a hand to take it, instability is implied. There need to be a clean hand-off from marketing to outside sales, then to inside sales, to operations, to service, and so on. Leaders create the relay environment and, if not successful in doing so, they risk losing the trust of their teams.

Trust is built at the handoff.

How can a leader build trust?

Leader has the responsibility of allowing people to be in an atmosphere that allows progression. That atmosphere, as with most of what we've discussed, comes from communication. The goal is to tear down walls between people, not build them up!

- Ask tough, deep questions of team members, because trust comes in when greater expectations are given
- Give time and patience to your team
- Be repetitive with those values and processes that make your company stable

UPbeat!

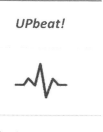

If a leader is too dialed into the present, how does the team know about the future?

- Adaptability is a necessity; the conversation can't be about how you've "always done things;" be open to new ideas to demonstrate respect for and reliability on the team.
- In team-building, the idea is not a "catch me so I don't fall," environment; rather, a team should live in such a way that they express the trust-building statement, "learn about me and understand how to work with me." Some people have trust; others have to have it earned.
- Trust is a proving ground. Use DISC assessments and have regular check-ins to confirm team trust.
- Compassion Stability and Hope, the other three factors to belonging, are built off of trust.

What happens when trust is not present?

When trust isn't present, neither is an engaged team. There's very little that can be done. The customers, being served by a disengaged team, are less likely to get products or services in the manner they see fit. If this becomes a pattern, the customer loses trust which, according to statistics, could also mean that the customer reduces or pulls away from the company entirely. If the company starts to fail as a result, the leader loses trust. This is the distrust cycle. The only way to break the cycle of distrust is to be purposeful about creating trust . . . and this generally starts with the leader.

What happens when trust is present?

When trust IS present, people want to go the extra mile. There is utter engagement from the team who, by serving in a fully engaged matter, create satisfied customers. Those customers begin to trust the company and may even become the people who refer other clients. The relationship built by that referral can create trust from the leadership in the customer, AND in the company. *With trust in the company, a leader is more likely to engage his team to provide trust and a sense of belonging.*

In the positive trust cycle, we do our best every single time knowing that others will do the same.

Record your own UPbeats on TRUST!

Looking for more on trust?

. . . So you have two people that don't trust each other and they cannot even tell each other that they don't trust each other. What do they do? Manufacturers set up more distributors and distributors add more lines to their arsenal. The distrust cycle starts...

So how do you stop it? How do you control this out of control cycle? There are a couple of simple things that you can do right away. Having been in this cycle at various times for thirty years now, I have seen some pretty crazy stuff go on. But I have also seen some very successful partnerships. Here are some keys to improving your relationship with your manufacturer or distributor . . .

Scan the code to read about the keys to trust on my blog at: http://positivepolarity.com/can-i-trust-you/.

Trust Reflection

Do yourself a favor and look at your best business relationships to see where the trust level is. Then look at your weakest business relationships and do the same.

Strategize with your in-house team on ways to improve your working relationship with your "partners."

Identify why the good relationships are working.

Objectively discern what is broken in the weaker relationships.

Meet with your customers, share your team's information with them, and let them know that you want to improve the relationship.

Compassion

If your team were asked whether a supervisor or someone in leadership at work cared about them as people, how do you think they'd respond?

When it comes to compassion, companies that value this principle:

- Are significantly more likely to keep employees with their organization.
- Have employees who take less sick days, work more hours, and have a more positive attitude.
- Will have more engaged customers.
- Are substantially more productive.
- Achieve greater profitability.

The larger a company is, the harder it is to foster an attitude of compassion because there is less interaction between all of the parties. Nonetheless, there are some simple ways to shine a light on the value of compassion.

Leadership needs to know when to enforce a rule and when to defend a team member. I remember an early job working in fast food where, as in many first jobs, we were trained that "the customer is always right." I had a customer order a one dollar soda, but through quick change artistry, he attempted to get more money in return than he'd given. I caught on, but the customer pulled back to punch me, so I gave him the money. This was not a case when the customer was right and, at the same time, my own safety could have been in danger. It was important for me to have a manager who had my back and, rather than scolding me for my drawer being off, sympathized with me over a no-win situation, but I had no defender that day. **Is your customer always right or does respect**

and compassion cover your team when they need or deserve those things?

Leaders should value quality of work as much as quantity of work. A friend of mine was with a company that gave an annual award for the number of hours worked and that award usually went to somebody working upwards of 3,500 hours per year, or around seventy hours per week for all fifty-two weeks of the year. Other people in the company were just as successful of producers and sellers, but this coveted award of "time in" was the company's most praised. What message was that company sending about compassion?

Leaders should arrange opportunities to serve—together as equals—in non-profit, educational, faith-based, or other volunteer or missional work or endeavors. One of the best team building events my company did was serving together. It was important for all levels of personnel. The more members of the team there serving, the better off the company is. Many companies make these service days paid work days to encourage involvement.

There comes a point in time in some companies when people become more important than profit and a day of service can redraw the lines of compassion in your company. In serving together, the team gets to see leaders in a non-leadership role, as comrades. (Consider even serving with an organization that has an entry-level employee in charge to give him or her an opportunity to shine.) This aspect of Servanthood helps to erase much of the "it's not my job," attitude that might exist in your workplace. The "Not My Job Department" is the enemy of compassion. Before your team's service day, a great motivator would be to find a video clip to share with your team to encourage working together. In my team, I used a scene from the movie MTV Paramount Pictures movie, "Coach

Carter." Scan the QR code above to go to https://www.youtube.com/watch?v=pLNLIHFSOYA and view this clip.

 By choosing to serve together, the whole team gets to see and work with a cause that, by its contrast, has the potential to highlight the blessing of work, and a paycheck, and your company. Volunteering together for a common cause can build your team in ways you might never have imagined. Compassion expressed through shared service and helping others brings a human perspective to a company.

Lastly, to develop and live by compassion, leaders should continue to reflect on the tough questions. There are times in life that we all get asked intense questions. These are the questions that, if used properly, can re-shape a life. When it comes to compassion, one of the four primary contributors to a sense of belonging, reflective questions (with honest answers) are an important driver to keep yourself accountable to the humanity aspect of the cold, corporate or professional world.

As a leader, whether in your family, or in your business, you get to answer one of these most important questions:

Do you want to be right, or do you want to be effective?

Is your daily life built around the concept of you having to be right, or is it built around you being effective? Before you answer this question for yourself, please take a minute or two and really reflect on what it is asking. Think about a few supporting questions:

Are you shutting down others without even knowing it?

Do you have a need for others to be wrong?

Do you feel like you are defending your position to others on a regular basis?

Are you often trying to prove your point to others?
Do you feel like it's your job to correct others regularly?

In business, here are a few things that could happen when you are always striving to be right:

- You will be seen as **arrogant**
- People will **resist** you.
- Some people will put up a **fight and argue** with you.
- You'll experience **passive-aggressiveness**.
- Your team could completely **shut down**.
- Ultimately, people **stop listening** entirely.

Just as much as you want your position to be respected and understood by others, the person that you are talking to wants the same thing. So why do you feel that, as a leader, you can take this posture of superiority? Would *you* want to be a follower of *you*? Maybe that is a better question to ask yourself.

"Would I want to follow me?"

You might be asking yourself what to do I do if you are more interested in being right than effective. As in most things in life, the first piece is to admit that you are a "right junkie!" If you are wondering if you are a "right junkie," ask someone close to you. If you've picked a good accountability partner, they will be honest with you and, if the answer is "yes," then you have some work to do. Start noticing that you would rather be right than effective. If you spend time working on being effective, then you will be able to more easily let someone else be right for a change.

Think positively about how you can let someone else share in the joy of being right today and imagine the ways that could lead to

UPbeat!

Would you want to be a follower of you? Maybe that is a better question to ask yourself.

better engagement. Remember in grade school, the feeling that comes when answering a question correctly in front of the whole class. Do your whole team a favor - go and find someone that needs to be right. Ask them a question that they are sure to get right. Then congratulate them on the answer and watch their day turn.

How many of us would like to be caught doing something right? Scan the QR code to the right to go to http://positivepolarity.com/catch-me-doing-something-right-please/to ponder on the idea of pointing out the positives on your team.

Building compassion into your organization is about building love into your organization so that your team and staff bring that love to the efforts they accomplish within it. How does one love something that doesn't have a heart? The heart of the organization is the leader. **Are you working for a bottom line or a cause? If it is a cause, are you leading in such a way that your team knows the answer and feels a sense of belonging to it?**

Record your own UPbeats on COMPASSION!

Looking for more on compassion?

Are you a "right junkie" in your business and looking for a way to both have compassion and handle the necessary and important business of what needs to be done? As a business owner, you may desire to lead with compassion, but also recognize that there are things that you are required to be "tough" about as a leader or owner. Where can you find balance?

> *. . . Has anyone ever called you a "control freak," or "controlling?" With as many things as are seemingly out of our control, it's no wonder that we want to control as much as we can! Now, shift your focus away from your personal life and focus on your business life for a second.*
>
> *As you think about business, the word "control" seems to lose its negativity, doesn't it?*
>
> *"Make sure to control your expenses."*
> *"Remember to control the sales process."*
> *"Who has the controlling shares in your business?"*
> *"When I am gone, you are in control."*
> *"We became profitable by being controlled."*
>
> *So now, let's look back at the first statement I made, "With as many things as are 'seemingly' out of control..." Are you aware of just how much you actually do control in your day-to-day business life . . .*

Scan the code to read about quenching your inner control freak at: http://positivepolarity.com/is-control-a-good-thing/.

Compassion Reflection

Remember these tough questions as you consider whether your company has created a family of compassion:

1. ***Do you want to be right, or do you want to be effective?***
2. Does your team believe they are cared about?
3. Do you enforce black and white rules and regulation more than compassion and understanding?
4. Do you allow respect and compassion to play parts in your assessment of staff to customer interactions?
5. Do you value quantity more than quality?
6. Do you serve together to show the heart of your organization?
7. Are you shutting others down?
8. Do you have a need for others to be wrong?
9. Do you spend a lot of time trying to defend or prove your own points or ideas?
10. Do you feel it's your job to correct others in your organization?
11. Have you ever been accused of arrogance?
12. Do you experience negative reactions such as: resistance, argument, passive aggressiveness, or a shutdown to listening or productivity?
13. Are you offering opportunities for others to lead and succeed in big ways such as service or smaller ways such as answering questions correctly in front of colleagues?
14. Are you working for a bottom line or a cause and is it clear to your team?
15. Would you want to follow you?

Stability

Team members who have confidence in their companies' financial futures are nine times more likely to be engaged in their jobs compared to those who do not have confidence in their organizations' financial future. By providing believable stability in your company, you are providing a pathway to engagement through confidence.

Recently, I got a postcard in the mail from my insurance carrier stating that it was time for me to check my cholesterol level. According to the literature, it was easy, free and they felt it was the right time. As I read this, I thought to myself, *'how do they know that it is the right time for this for me?' Define "easy"... it might be for them, but how do I know that it is easy for me? Why do they even care? I'm a bit scared, since I don't know what is involved or what they could find.'*

I was left with more questions than answers.

What does this have to do with business? Before I answer that, let's imagine that you are working hard at your desk when there is a knock on your door. You look at your schedule and see that there is nothing scheduled at this time, so your curiosity peaks as you get up and walk toward the door. Through the opaque glass you see a figure, but you cannot tell who it is. As your hand reaches out to open the door, you hesitate for a moment. *'What if it's not good news?'* you think to yourself; for an instant, you freeze, now wishing the person would go away.

'Get a grip!' you tell yourself.

As you open the door, you see that it is your best client and a sudden sense of relief comes over you, but wait; why is he here? As you greet him, you think to yourself, *'was I supposed to have this meeting and it did not get on my calendar?'* After exchanging the normal pleasantries, you ask him how you can help him. He stalls when the topic comes up. *'This can't be good,'* you think to yourself. *'Did he come over here to yell at me? Or worse yet, fire me?'*

"You know," he says, "I have always been your best advocate both to my team and to anyone that would listen to me. But lately, there have been a few things that have caused me to look at our business relationship and take notice."

For the next thirty minutes your "best client" proceeds to tell you all of the things that he thought could help your business. After he leaves, you sit back in your chair and really think about what he said. *'Why did I not catch these?'* you ask yourself.

Typically, this would not happen. More often than not, your clients want you to figure out where your business needs strengthening. Most clients do not have the time or the expertise to tell you how to improve your business.

An effective leader will ask himself these questions:

- When is the right time to do a business checkup?
- Will it be easy?
- Who will even notice if I do this?
- What if I find things I don't want to know?

All of these are great questions, but in the end, when would you rather know the answers to these questions? Do you want to have the answers today, when you can still do something about them, or later, when the choices are far less desirable or fixable? Do yourself, your business, your team, and your clients a favor and check on your business today. Provide the stability that all of your company's entities are seeking.

There are three powerful things that a leader can do for a provision of stability.

1 - Create a vision. Running a company without a vision is like golfing without a hole. Begin with a personal vision by asking the question, 'If money wasn't an object, what would I do with my life?' How closely does that vision line up with the work of your business or with what can be accomplished as a result of success in your work?

Accept that visions may change and allow the team to be a part of those changes. If they are a part of creating that vision, then they will have buy-in to it and engagement in making it a reality. Scan the code to read about goal-setting to put you in the right frame of mind for developing your company's vision. The original blog is found at: http://positivepolarity.com/to-do-goals-vs-to-be-goals/.

Don't have an asterisk for "whatever it takes" in your company's pursuit of vision if you are seeking true stability. *'I'm responsible for twenty-two families,'* is how I used to look at my work. I would see the families at parties and events and I knew it was up to me to pay those families' bills. This meant that I couldn't say I'll do whatever it takes to get the customers we need to make payroll:

- . . . with the exception of working long hours.
- . . . unless it means I have to do the menial tasks.
- . . . only when the economy is doing great.

On that golf course, you don't stop playing when the ball goes in the weeds; it just might take an extra stroke or two to make it to the hole. The same must be true for your business. Whatever it takes to make that vision a reality is what you must do to create stability in the eyes of your fellow leadership, your team, and your clients.

2 - Bring what you can to the table as a leader including:

- Time investment – Be available beyond administration and production; be available for communications.
- Knowledge – Become and maintain the expert leadership position in your company so that your team feels confident in your ability.
- Relationships – With team members and with other businesses, build relationships which go deeper than names and titles; know about your people and be open to letting them know a little bit about you.

3 - Create an environment of transparency. The team needs to see that the leader is as vulnerable as the team. Both with the team and in personal actions in the workplace, the leader should address issues head-on. A stable company doesn't allow:

1. Ignoring of issues related to finance, process, production or client relationships
2. Avoidance of inner or outer conflict
3. Fakeness or dishonesty

Without stability, companies experience higher turnover, loss of longevity, and drops in morale. Given the simplicity of three leadership steps to growing stability—vision, leadership skills, and transparency—it is the ideal piece for leaders to begin at as they work toward building a sense of belonging in their organizations.

Record your own UPbeats on STABILITY!

Looking for more on stability?

When you think of stability, it's rare that the word, "change," would come to mind. In reality, though, change is necessary for stability. Your team and clients need to see that you are always looking forward in order to have confidence in the stability of your enterprise. Planning forward will usually require an element of change. In other words, contrary to it being a step-sibling to stability, change is actually its twin.

> *. . . How many times have you done things that you really did not want to do? How did it turn out? Typically, when your heart and soul are not in something, the success is significantly less than when you are committed to it completely.*
>
> *Let's look at change for a moment—who likes change? Who fears change? Who would rather go to the dentist and get teeth pulled without Novocain? If you said "yes" to any of these, then join the club. Why so fearful? Why is it so hard to change?*
>
> *Think of something you want to change in your life. Let's say you want to go to the gym and workout more. There are four stages of readiness that, if looked at properly, will help you see where you are at and why you do what you do . . .*

Scan the code to read about preparing for change at: http://positivepolarity.com/are-you-ready/.

Stability Reflection

We mentioned several things that a leader can bring to a table in his or her business including: time investment, knowledge, and relationships. Uniquely, you likely have other very specific things that you could bring, as a leader, to your team, your company, and your clients. Think about and note what those things might be.

To my company, I bring . . .

To my team, I bring . . .

To my clients, I bring . . .

Hope

How would you answer this question: "Does my company's leadership make me feel enthusiastic about the future?" How would your team answer it? And how would you feel if you knew that sixty-nine percent of employees surveyed who said "yes" to this question are engaged at work; by comparison, of those who answered "no" in the same Gallup poll, only one percent were considered to be engaged in their work. Who wouldn't want to affect a nearly seventy percent swing in engagement with their company? I guess the real question is *how* could one affect such a positive dramatic change for your company?

Hopelessness is a powerful contributor to a stressful work environment and stress is the ultimate hidden productivity killer in the workplace. When it comes to stress, employees—whether consciously or not—ask themselves routinely whether the energy that they put into their jobs is equal to the rewards that they're getting out . . . or not. If those levels are not in balance, the employees do not have hope. They will have disbelief in the future and the future is all about hope.

Sixty-six percent of employees report that they have difficulty focusing on tasks and end goals at work because of stress. Stress has been called the "health epidemic of the twenty-first century" by the World Health Organization and its estimated to cost American businesses is as much as three hundred BILLION per year.

Contact me to ask about having a stress assessment completed with your organization. Scan the code at the right or visit me at: http://positivepolarity.com/contact-us/.

Why is the stress epidemic so dangerous where business is concerned? Let's look at some statistics to get to the root of this growth stunting issue:

- 40% of workers reported their job was very or extremely stressful
- 25% view their jobs as the number one stressor in their lives
- 75% of employees believe that workers have more on-the-job stress than a generation ago
- 80% of workers feel stress on the job, nearly half say they need help in learning how to manage stress and 42% say their coworkers need such help
- 25% have felt like screaming or shouting because of job stress
- In other words, stress is the health epidemic and the workplace is its breeding ground. When employees put those two things together, which do you think will be

sacrificed: health or work? The answer is not to have employees put work before health, but rather to make work a healthier (and less stressful) place to be.

Let's look deeper at the ways in which stress manifest itself in professional environments. The main stressors at work come from:

- Improbable Demands
- Unequal Balance Between Efforts and Rewards
- A Feeling of Being Controlled (or Having no control)
- Organizational Change
- Inept Managers or Supervisors (or Bad Relationships with Managers or Supervisors)
- Lack of Social Support
- Uncertain Job Security

One solution for leaders would be to supply one of these with each employee on-boarding packet:

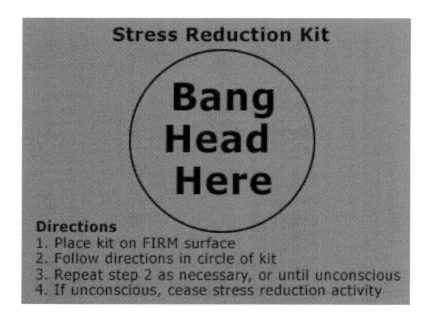

Stress Reduction Kit

Bang
Head
Here

Directions
1. Place kit on FIRM surface
2. Follow directions in circle of kit
3. Repeat step 2 as necessary, or until unconscious
4. If unconscious, cease stress reduction activity

Before the hidden costs of stress, consider instead breaking down the seven stressors of the workplace. Do you see the stressor in your teams? Is it justified (healthy) stress? If not, can the stress be managed with coping mechanisms for an individual employee, or is there a real issue that should be handled by leadership – a purposeful effort to reduce the stressor in order to reduce the stress in his or her employees?

Demands

Demands, when appropriate to the employee's role, are not a bad thing; they actually help us to cope and develop new strategies for engagement. Moreover, they can provide a feeling of purposefulness to the employee. Naturally, as the workplace stress increases, so too do demands. If employees are reacting stressfully to the demands of their workplaces, there are three areas leaders should take a second look at:

1. Is the role a poorly designed job?
2. Is the workload excessive?
3. Are the talents matching the tasks?

Looking at the role of demands on stress in the workplace, how would you measure your own professional environment? Do you need a change in job design, workload, or task to talent matching?

Effort/Reward Balance

Purpose and job satisfaction are vital to success at work. Without reward of some kind, the high effort will become a stressor in our lives. Effort needs to match the reward. A reward can be in the form of a higher base compensation or a bonus for a major completed project. Sometimes, the effort could warrant promotion to another role that maintains a task to talent match for the employee. However, these tangible and sometimes unaffordable rewards are only part of the picture.

Employees also feel reward in the form of:
1. Recognition
2. Personal growth
3. Helping others succeed

The questions leaders should pose to themselves are: 1) Is my team being rewarded? 2) Do the rewards match the efforts they put forth? 3) What types of rewards motivate my team and are those the ones I am using to create an Effort/Reward Balance?

Each person is different. Find out what rewards motivate your whole team and the individuals within your team.

Contact me to ask about having a DISC assessment completed with your organization. Scan the code at the right or visit me at: http://positivepolarity.com/contact-us/.

Control

Feeling powerless is a universal cause of job stress. Not every person will have a say in how operations work in every part of the company. Nonetheless, each team member needs to feel some sense of control over those things that they know and do in the workplace. They also need to feel they are in appropriate communication with those who do have control over their roles. If leaders want to know the answer as to whether their team feels powerless, consider these twin questions to the same concern:

- Do you feel like no one hears you?
- Do you feel misunderstood at work?

"Yes" answers to these questions could indicate that there is a control stressor in place for those employees.

There are some realities to the roles of employees versus those of leaders. Some positions will, by their nature, have less authority and responsibility in the day-to-day activities. When those responsibilities do increase, so must the amount of control that team member has. This balance between responsibility and authority is as vital as that between effort and rewards when it comes to stress.

UPbeat!

This balance between responsibility and authority is as vital as that between effort and reward when it comes to stress.

Organizational Change

A recent study showed that seventy-five percent of workers do not think that their mission statement is actually the way they do business. The same survey showed that companies whose employees understand the mission and goals enjoy a twenty-nine percent greater return than other firms. If there is a misalignment, between a mission or vision and the way business is done, one of two things needs to . . . CHANGE. (That is the scary word, here.): Change the way you do business, or change the business mission.

The reality about change is that it produces uncertainty. Some employees may thrive on the energy of the unknown; most do not. Most are stressed out by change.

When it comes to organizational change, in order to prevent it from becoming a stressor to one's team, a leader should ensure that the change is accompanied by:

1. Organizational Communication – Make sure the team and leadership are all aware of the specifics of the change: what will change, when will it change, who will be affected, and how do we communicate these things most effectively.

2. Organizational Evolution – Change should not be arbitrary; the company needs to be constantly growing and evolving with its industry trends. Change must be purposeful. It's the kiss of death to a company when its leaders say that they do things a certain way simply because "we've always done things that *way* around here."

3. Organizational Vision – Change should either align with the company's vision or the vision should be addressed to ensure it aligns with the company change.

When it comes to change, particularly as it aligns with a company's vision, do not be confused in thinking that a company is able to haphazardly change its vision with the wind of a new fad. However, a leader must accept that a changing vision may be necessary to maintain a competitive advantage in his or her market space.

For instance, consider the current mission statement for the popular online streaming service, Netflix®:

> *"Our core strategy is to grow our streaming subscription business domestically and globally. We are continuously improving the customer experience, with a focus on expanding our streaming content, enhancing our user interface and extending our streaming service to even more Internet-connected devices, while staying within the parameters of our consolidated net income and operating segment contribution profit targets."*

Prior to the revolution of streaming, though, Netflix® didn't have a mission statement at all! What it had, instead, were a vision, a promise, and nine values that could not be summed up in a more succinct way than:

Our vision for the future includes:
- *Becoming the best global entertainment distribution service*
- *Licensing entertainment content around the world*
- *Creating markets that are accessible to film makers*
- *Helping content creators around the world to find a global audience*

We promise our customers stellar service, our suppliers a valuable partner, our investors the prospects of sustained profitable growth, and our employees the allure of huge impact.

Netflix® is a perfect example of change that was absolutely necessary. Without the change from DVD distribution to a streaming service, they would have gone the way of Blockbuster®. Furthermore, the mission statement still embodied its first point for the future which was to become the best global entertainment distribution service. Merely the platform through which they accomplished distribution changed . . . because the WORLD changed!

Change is, without a doubt, one of the biggest stressors of the work environment, but it is *not* a stressor that can be avoided if a company is to continue growing, evolving, and staying profitable. It is not up to a leader to avoid change, rather he or he should be careful to communicate its necessity, be true to a company's vision, and choose purposeful change.

Manager/Supervisor

Reasonable directives from leadership are expected by employees and team members. If an employee is experiencing stress, for instance, because he or she is being asked to arrive on time, the problem is not on the leader. A clock-requiring job may not be the right fit for the employee. "Reasonable" is a subjective definition, though, and it is on the company's leadership to decide what is reasonable and what is not. The leader must then work to create buy-in . . . and not create waves.

Consider these three questions for employees with regard to stress caused by their managers or supervisors:

- Does your leader support you?
- How often do you agree with leadership?
- Do you follow because you have to or want to?

If employees are feeling unsupported, disagreeable, and forced into compliance on a regular basis, this stressor is likely to be on leadership to fix, rather than on the employee.

Social Support

An unsupportive environment from others can cause stress in the lives of a leader's team. That stress could be coming from those under the employee in the hierarchy, such as when an employee is having to deal repeatedly with problems because a leader has a fear of replacing an entry-level person who is not performing. Stress can come from employees working side-by-side when one person is pulling more of the workload, there is a personality conflict, or recognition is not evenly doled out. The stress of unsupportiveness can also trickle down to employees from above.

In the contemporary workplace, colleagues often see one another as friends and family, emotionally speaking. While there is a job that must get done, it's important to recognize the importance of social support in order to prevent the stress that comes when it is missing. As a leader, determine boundaries regarding relationships and communications (and enforce them equally). Make your professional environment a positive place to be, by discouraging negativity. Be a part of the solution of positivity through encouragement, recognition, and sincere expressions of concern when appropriate.

Job Security

For some employees, it may be impossible for their leaders to erase this stress, as it is fear-based. The uncertainty of unemployment is a justifiably scary place for grown adults. Leaders need to be cautious about two opposing actions (or inactions, as it were) that represent the biggest contributors to the stressor of job security:

1. Lack of advancement
2. Promoting too fast or too slow

How to Reduce Stress in the Work Environment

Whether the leader, an employee, or a leader working with an employee, there are some simple steps that can be taken to create a lower stress environment in the workplace. These steps are helpful for all seven of the primary professional stressors.

1. Act rather than react in the workplace. Having controls in place that are enforced is easier than having to clean up from uncontrolled situations.
2. On the note of control, control what you can (*your* actions and responses) and not what you can't.
3. Take a deep breath:
   - Inhale for five seconds
   - Hold for five seconds
   - Exhale for five seconds
4. Reduce interruptions – ask others for help in this matter
   - Turn off your emails
   - Turn off your cell phones
   - Schedule uninterrupted time

5. Schedule rest every ninety minutes, following a period of intense concentration.
   - Walk
   - Stretch
6. Leaders and employees alike should watch for self-imposed stress through some reflecting questions and proven rituals.
   - Are you generally a negative person?
   - Is the cup half full or half empty?
   - When is enough wealth really enough?
   - Sit up straight
   - Get organized
   - Abandon unrealistic goals

"Stop focusing on how stressed you are and remember how blessed you are"

~Unknown

Why so much about stress? Stress is the antithesis of hope and hope is the last, essential key to creating a sense of belonging in your team.

It is so helpful for us, as business leaders, to look back at the year and review both our successes and our . . . let's call them "not-so-successes." We long to look back and give ourselves a pat on the back for what we did right, whether it was goals we met, accomplishments we made, or personal lives we helped to change for the better, based on professional provisions.

We should also look back and see what things we could do better *in the future*. Reflection is kind of like the "in memoriam" slideshows at the end of every year that goes through the list of celebrities who died. As we reflect on the loss, we remember them for all the good things they did in the world while they were here. Contrarily, future is all about hope.

hope (noun):
the feeling that what is wanted can be had
or that events will turn out for the best.

Our approach to reflection is the same way we need to regard looking forward and the things that we have yet to accomplish. Start with the "not-so-successes" of the last years. Some may call them failures, but could you possibly consider them goals not yet realized? Whatever they are, consider whether they are still relevant and whether the goals need to be readjusted.

Readjustment is vital. Learning from your mistakes is a free lesson that may cost a lot on the front end, but can pay dividends over the long haul when you apply the hard-earned lessons. Readjusted failures can become new goals. I strongly encourage my clients to have "To Do" goals (tasks) and "To Be" goals (behaviors) as touched upon when discussing vision planning and stability.

Goals that are not made are sometimes found to be:

- **Unrealistic**
- **Unprepared**
- **Unmotivated**

Focusing on behaviors rather than tasks is a much more exciting way to accomplish goals. What we're all looking for are results, which come from behavioral changes and not from the completing of tasks.

Goals and vision help to unify a team around hope, but those pieces are merely one piece of the tangible roadmap to an intangible feeling. How else can you build the elusive sentiment of hope? Because hope is a human emotion, leaders should seek to build a human perspective into their businesses. To create a tangible roadmap to the intangible sense of hope, tie together task and behavior goals.

1. DECREASE stress in the workplace (Tasks and Behaviors, as reviewed)
2. Build enthusiasm for the future through a vision and goals. (Behavior)
3. Give roles to each person en route to those goals so that each feels a sense of contribution. (Task)
4. Create anticipation for the reward at the finish line repeatedly and with detail to entice each type of personality on your team. (Behavior)
5. Require a team-centric environment wherein each person is expected to help the other, and also know that their colleagues would help them in turn. (Task)

Knowing that things can and will stay positive, or, be better in the future is a powerful motivator. Few things, as much as hope, can encourage a sense of belonging. Hope propels people during difficult times, increases productivity, promotes teamwork, and encourages empowerment.

Record your own UPbeats on HOPE!

Looking for more on hope?

Stress focuses on worries about the future. Hope focuses on excitement for the future. The future of a company, determined through vision and a plan, is developed and communicated by a leader. By planning ahead, a leader is really planning to build hope into his or her team and building hope builds a sense of belonging

UPbeat!

Stress focuses on worries about the future. Hope focuses on excitement for the future.

. . . There are a lot of people who say, "This is the way it is around here," or, "That's the way we've always done it" and they have no interest in thinking outside the box.

And we hear 'thinking outside the box,' so often now, that that has become the box.

So, we have to look at our businesses and really ask ourselves, "Is this what we want? Is this really the growth we want to see?" We have to ask ourselves . . .

Scan the code to watch the video, "That Was Yesterday" to challenge your thinking on hope, change, and planning for the future at: http://positivepolarity.com/that-was-yesterday/.

Hope Reflection

Ask yourself whether your workplace is an environment of STRESS, worry for the future, or an environment of HOPE, excitement for the future.

What stresses can you help to remove to decrease the workplace's negativity?

What hope can you help to build to increase the workplace's positivity?

Migrating to the
Communication Comfort Zone

Can You Talk?

*Dành cho khách hàng công nghiệp, các
khu vực lớn nhất của mối quan tâm đối với
quan hệ tin cậy là một mức độ rất thấp
của giao tiếp. Theo cuộc điều tra, sáu
mươi ba phần trăm của nhà phân phối và
bảy mươi ba phần trăm của các nhà sản
xuất cho thấy rằng chất lượng cao hai
cách giao tiếp là hầu như không tồn tại.*

There are 6,500 languages in the world and 2,000 of those have less than 1,000 speakers. Within the various languages, there are multiple versions and dialects adding up to tens of thousands of ways to say, "hello," among millions of other sentiments beyond a greeting. Given the enormity of our modern day Tower of Babel, how many times in a conversation are we apt to ask, *'what?'*

Our communication styles are as varied as languages. When we don't speak or communicate with attention to emotional quotients or personality types, we risk being as misunderstood as if I were to break out into Vietnamese. Unless you had some fluency in Vietnamese, you wouldn't know that what I said above was: *for industrial clients, the greatest area of concern with regard to relational trust is an extremely low level of communication.*

According to the survey, sixty-three percent of distributors and seventy-three percent of manufacturers indicate that high quality two-way communication is virtually non-existent.

To come full circle on our team building, look back at those personality types discovered in our two question employee surveys. The "A" of team-strengthening is to "Acknowledge Thyself." That acknowledgment is about having self-awareness *in order to* be better in one's approach to communications. If we start going in a conversation and don't check in along the way, we could lose people because we're not speaking in their styles; we're not speaking their languages. We need to pay attention to the other people coming into sync with what we are saying.

Communication is a dance. when you dance, you both have to take steps. The speaker has the responsibility of making sure the listener is understanding. The listener has the responsibility to ask for help when he or she is *not* understanding. Each dancer must migrate into the zone of the other in order to achieve smooth movements.

UPbeat!

Sixty-three percent of distributors and seventy-three percent of manufacturers indicate that high quality two-way communication is virtually non-existent.

Communication Migration Steps:

1. Use the two question survey to determine whether you should:
    a. Speak quickly or at a measured pace.
    b. Focus on facts or relationships.
2. Determine whether the person you are speaking to is a visual, auditory, or kinesthetic learner. The simple

question to determine this answer is: "Would you prefer I just tell you 'such-and-such,' do you want to learn as you go, or would you like some printed information?"

   a. Your visual learners like to SEE things written – including graphic representations of data. Your auditory learners will want to HEAR you speak about a topic. Your kinesthetic learners will want to learn by DOING.

3. After discovering the personality style and the learning style, become a chameleon; MIGRATE TO THE LISTENER'S COMMUNICATION COMFORT ZONE.

Contact me to ask about having a DISC assessment completed with your organization. Scan the code at the right or visit me at: http://positivepolarity.com/contact-us/.

A leader's downfall is when he or she begins to believe that communication is about telling. In reality, communication is about sharing together. Two people who are unwilling to budge from their communication zones can result in conflict. When there is conflict, the communicators tend to dig their feet in deeper, solidifying the gap between one another's communication differences. The culmination is often the necessity for conflict resolution.

Conflict Resolution:

Whenever you're in conflict with someone, there is one factor that can make the difference between damaging your relationship and deepening it. That factor is attitude.

—William James

The cost of conflict in the U.S. is estimated at thirty percent of managers' time and three hundred fifty-nine billion dollars annually. While there is constructive conflict that can result in positive outcomes such as mutually shared decisions, equality in the workplace, and strong, honest relationships, more often than not, professional conflict is destructive.

The results of workplace conflict include:

- High Turnover
- Sick Days
- Poor Outcome
- Poor Productivity
- Aggressive Behavior
- Tension
- Avoidance
- Stress

Before conflict has those outcomes, though, good leaders can recognize it early when they see employees or team members who:

- Shut Down
- Blame Others
- Have Poor Communication with Others
- Are Stressed Around Specific Individuals
- Lack a Desire for Teamwork
- Unjustifiably Complain
- "Backstab" or "Throw" Fellow Workers "Under the Bus"

- Deny Responsibility for Failures
- Are Selfish
- Present as Victimized
- Lie
- Are Fearful
- Are Critical of Others
- Behave Aggressively

Conflict is going to occur in any environment with people, working together. People have different points of view. People have different communication styles. People spend large amounts of time together. People depend on one another to get the job done. People have their own agendas. People have their own expectations. People have their own needs. It's a wonder we can accomplish anything at all with the amount of inherent conflict that exists between two individuals. These different needs wanted by individuals really boil down to our very human desires for power, control, freedom, expression, safety, dignity, happiness, support, and flexibility.

When it comes to conflict:

DO	DON'T
Understand that conflict is inevitable – it will happen!	Focus on personality traits that cannot be changed.
Resolve to address the conflict quickly – what happens when we don't?	Interrupt.
Focus on the problem, not the parties.	Attack.
Acknowledge how the parties are feeling.	Disregard the feelings of others.

Listen actively to both parties.	Avoid the conflict.
Use constructive conflict behaviors.	Allow emotions to take over the conversation.
Follow a conflict resolution process.	Impose your personal values or beliefs.

Constructive Conflict Behaviors

- Listening
- Innovation
- Empathy
- Strategy
- Respect
- Flexibility
- Shared Goals
- Movement Forward
- Win/Win Solutions
- Compromising
- Open

The Six Steps to the Conflict Resolution Process

1. Clarify what the disagreement is.
2. Establish a common goal for both parties.
3. Discuss ways to meet the common goal.
4. Determine the barriers to the common goal.
5. Agree on the best way to resolve the conflict.
6. Acknowledge the agreed upon solution and determine the responsibilities each party has in the resolution.

This process should be completed by all parties in the conflict together.

Clarify what the disagreement is

Clarifying involves getting to the heart of the conflict. The goal of this step is to get both sides to agree on what the disagreement is.

Tips:

- Discuss what needs are not being met on both sides of the conflict. Ensure mutual understanding.

- Obtain as much information as possible on each side's point of view.

- Continue to ask questions until you are certain that you and each side of the conflict understand the issue.

Establish a common goal for both parties

In this step of the process, both sides agree on the desired outcome of the conflict.

Tips:

- Discuss what each party would like to see happen.

- Find some common ground in both sides as a starting point for a shared outcome. That commonality can be as simple as both sides wanting to end the conflict.

Discuss ways to meet the common goal

Both sides work together to discuss ways that they can meet the goal they agreed upon in the second step.

Tips:

- Brainstorm different approaches to meet the goal.
- Discuss approaches until all the options are exhausted.

- Present compromise and buy-in as the themes of the discussion.

Determine the barriers to the common goal

In this step of the process, the two parties acknowledge what has brought them into the conflict.

Tips:

- Ask: "If we could have the outcome that we both wanted, how would that look?"
- Define what can (and what cannot) be changed about the situation.
- For the items that cannot be changed, discuss ways of getting around those road blocks.
- For the items that can be changed, brainstorm manners of change.

Agree on the best way to resolve the conflict

Both parties come to a conclusion on the best resolution.

Tips:

- Determine a solution that both sides can live with.
- Discuss the responsibility each party has in maintaining the solution.
- Settle on a means of ensuring that this conflict does not arise again.

Acknowledge the agreed upon solution and determine the responsibilities each party has in the resolution

Both sides own their responsibility in the resolution of the conflict and express aloud what they have agreed to.

Tips:

- Get both parties to acknowledge a win-win situation.
- Ask both parties to use phrases such as "I agree to..." and "I acknowledge that I have responsibility for..."
- Build in accountability and benchmarks to prevent future or repeated conflict around the same issues.

Recently, I was working with a large group of leaders on the topic of communication. I warned them from the start that the information that they were about to see was not difficult to learn; in fact, most of them already knew everything I was about to share.

A sense of confusion came over the group. Within the first five minutes of the presentation, I watched as the confusion turned to guilt. We were discussing some very elementary, foundational, communication truths . . . and they were not doing them.

Approximately eighty-five percent of our success is due, not to our education, our commitment or our ambition, but rather to how well we communicate. Many people struggle with things such as: not interrupting others, forming an opinion before hearing all of the facts, sharing personal agendas before finding out the needs of those to whom they are talking, convincing (manipulating) others rather than getting buy-in, and staying positive.

How well you are doing with this list of communication struggles?

Communication skills are not taught to us in school. It's often just assumed that we're born with all of this knowledge already built into us. Is it possible, though, that the

UPbeat!

Approximately eighty-five percent of our success is due, not to our education, our commitment, or our ambition, but rather to how well we communicate.

opposite is true? What if we are naturally built with the need to interrupt, with the tendency to form an opinion early on in a discussion, and with a struggle to stay positive at all times.

With countless languages, broken up by countless dialects, expressed in visual, auditory, and kinesthetic ways and interpreted according to various personality types, it takes work to be good at communicating properly. Nonetheless, most of us assume that others will acclimate to our style. This approach is potentially dangerous to our thinking. We all sell something, even if it's just an opinion. To assume that our listeners will just put their needs aside, and their personalities aside, to go with our ideas, is something that can get us into deep trouble with conflict and more.

When we migrate to the communication comfort zone of others, we are exemplifying compassion, one of the components to creating a sense of belonging; and, if we are to be able to migrate to another's communication comfort zone, we must acknowledge our own.

Strengthening a team is about strengthening the leader through the ABC's:

A.CKNOWLEDGE Thyself

Create a Sense of **B.ELONGING**

Migrate to the **C.OMMUNICATION** Comfort Zone

A strong team . . . is just the beginning of a stellar customer experience . . . and growing on purpose.

Record your own UPbeats on the ABCs of Leadership!

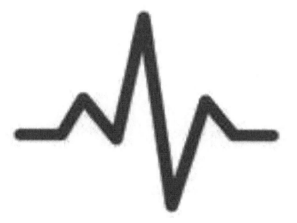

Part 2:

Improving Your Customer Experience

Peace is not absence of conflict, it is the ability to handle conflict by peaceful means.
–Ronald Reagan

The External D's

Your Customer's Experience

According to recent research, eighty percent of executives think customer satisfaction is more important than it was just three years ago and ninety-five percent of business leaders see it as the next competitive battleground.

The first step . . . the first "D" of improving customer experience is to know that you want to do it. What does it take for a leader to look deeper at customer experience? The "aha moment" could be the loss of a client, a missed opportunity, or even a bad survey result. Something must get a leader to question, *'How good is our customer experience . . . really . . . and what can we do about it?'*

UPbeat!

Decide

When I was working to build my company, I discovered that our particular product was not particularly unique; in fact, there were more than a hundred other places in the local vicinity to buy our product. The only way to create

The offering needs to go beyond the product.

success was to improve our *offering*. The offering needs to go beyond the product.

We were limited in our knowledge, so we brought our clients in to share what they knew. They were called our "customer council." They got a title and felt like they were (*and actually were*) a part of the process.

Because, as with different personalities and needs on the team, there were different desires among our customers, we began to customize our product packages. We made a list of all of the customized offerings and allowed the clients to choose. Customization is far from routine; accomplishing it requires an engaged team . . . that's why you start with strengthening the team.

In many companies, they desire creating a positive customer experience ONLY IF:

- It doesn't cost money.
- It doesn't cost time.
- It doesn't cost energy.
- It doesn't cost change.
- It doesn't cost convenience.

During our "customer council" meetings, not only was the company learning, but the clients were learning from one another, AND getting a free networking event. We became the connector for our clients. I spent more of my day trying to connect others and grow their businesses than my own. (Consequently, my own business growth was a natural result.) We also became a trusted coaching resource to our clients.

Leaders need to ask their clients the question: "How can we help?"

Teaching things that your clients need that maybe aren't even your specialty area and require some outside resources, could be the difference between your clients seeing you as a partner, or as *just another bill to pay.*

*Those who work their land will have abundant food,
but those who chase fantasies will have their fill of
poverty.*

~*Proverbs 28:19*

We can control what goes on in our immediate area (and not very far beyond). The goal is to have an experience that is positive, because the better it is, the more likely people will want to engage with it. If leaders don't make the decision to provide a quality customer experience, the decision will be made for them. In business, you're gonna live or you're gonna die. DECIDE!

Determine

We had to determine the ability of our team to fulfill the expressed needs of our clients. We became leaders that others followed. We also became innovators that could require more of our vendors and provide more value to clients who were willing to pay for the level of quality service we provided.

There are customer service departments in many companies, but – honestly – everybody needs to be serving the customer. You must determine your service ability based on your internal team.

UPbeat!

There are customer service departments in many companies, but – honestly – everybody needs to be serving the customer.

Two fundamental truths take center stage when focusing on the determination to provide a quality customer experience:

1. Everybody's job is customer service, and
2. There are NO winners of the "it's not my job" game.

Imagine a work atmosphere in which everybody says, "I'll do some." (Remember *Coach Carter*?)

DETERMINE!

Design

Design needs to come from a cross section of customers, vendors, and team members; it's a network creating a joint effort toward quality service. Providing an experience without a plan is akin to trying to build a house without a set of blueprints. Use a combination of personal experiences that are negative (to avoid repeating) and positive (to emulate) in order to create an improved customer interaction.

Pre-conceived notions keep architects of a customer service plan in the box. Open mindedness is essential to the success of any design. The complete customer experience should be intentional, not by mistake. DESIGN!

Define and Deliver

Roughly two thirds of lost clients leave due to a poor customer experiences and only one third leave because of cost, competition, or other reasons. If you're dialed into your client and looking at the two thirds piece, you'll continue to grow.

When it comes to delivery:

- Define realistic expectations for the task.
- Bring trust, compassion, stability, and hope to the experience.
- Have accountability to the purpose.

UPbeat!

With two-thirds of our customers' decisions to stay based on the customer experiences we provide, there is no excuse for not holding onto our clients.

With two-thirds of our customers' decisions to stay based on the customer experiences we provide, there is no excuse for not holding onto our clients. DEFINE and DELIVER!

The deliverable should be specific in the customer experience. There are three ways that a leader can ensure the delivery's success:

1. **Micromanage** – Assign the task, but stay over the workers' shoulders the entire time, and directing each step of the process or production; after all, you're the leader. Who could do it better?

2. **Let the Inmates Run the Asylum** – Hand off the task in the hopes that the team will accomplish according to the necessary specifications; after all, you're the leader. You can't be bothered with menial tasks.

3. **Find the Middle** – Assign the task with specifically outlined objectives and make yourself available (your time, your knowledge, your relationships) through the fulfillment of the deliverable; don't forget, you're the leader. They look to you for guidance and support.

A team hears the need for quality customer service best when it is coming from the middle.

How does the team deliver the experience? Through guidance and support . . . people want empowerment.

Dare to Differ

Work on the business, not just in it.

Visualize the short term AND the long term goals, as well as what it will take to get there

Evaluate the short term and long term *mission* routinely.

Be willing to change; there are many new things under the sun.

"Don't reinvent the wheel" is a misnomer.

Did you know that, if you take off by plane in Milwaukee for San Diego, and you are off by just four degrees north, you would end up in Los Angeles? SMALL course corrections can make a huge difference; the same is true for business. Don't be afraid to change things up for success.

Once a leader has *decided* on the necessity of quality customer service, *determined* the needs of the client, as well as the team to fulfill the service, *designed* an offering, *defined* the *delivery*, and found *differing* ways to flex the offering to clients, what kind of a return can he or she expect?

How do all of the D's look in action when it comes to the customer experience?

Reward for a great job with a client is not necessarily financial in the short term. In fact, good customer service might actually come at a higher cost, initially. Good service, thought, is the thing that will make a client more likely to recommend you to a friend or other business leader. Also, good service can create a forgiving atmosphere in the event of a mistake, including those mistakes that are the result of subcontractors or others.

Relationship-centered service, as opposed to just cold delivery, builds forgiveness and second chances. A merciful environment allows a business relationship to grow, become a repeating source of revenue, and ultimately set your company up to be the support when a client becomes successful.

As a general rule, as much as it is cultural to verbally deny it, we are negative communicators. One Gallup poll measured parents' focus on children's best grade to their worst grade. "Your child shows the following grades: Englilsh – A, Social Studies, A, Biology – C, Algebra – F; which grade deserves the most attention from you?" In the U.S., seven percent focused on the A's, while seventy-seven percent focused on the F's.

Remember, others respond with negative reinforcement, as well. According to an American Express survey, when it comes to customer service, negative messages travel exponentially further (and more often) than positive messages, particularly in our social media society.

- 1 unhappy customer will tell 9 others
- 13% of unhappy customers will tell 20 others
- Only 1 out of 20 will let the business know that they are unhappy

In other words, often without the leader ever even realizing it, there could be a strong current of dissatisfaction being sent out into the world. However, the statistics on the other side of complaints are something by which to be encouraged.

- 70% of clients return to a business if a complaint is resolved.
- 95% of clients return to a business if it resolves a complaint *quickly*.

Improving Customer Service

You know you *must* improve customer service, but how? This is where the two parts – leader and team – need to be strong. It will take an engaged team, and a leader who guides and supports them, to make customer service as good as it should be.

Clients leave. It's a fact of business. However, clients tend to leave, more than anything else, because of a lack of personalized, emotional customer service:

- 1% Die
- 3% Move Away
- 5% Were "Lured" Away by a Friend
- 9% Were "Lured Away by a Competitor
- 14% Were Disappointed with the Product
- 68% of Customers Leave as the Result of an Indifferent Attitude Perceived from the Company Toward the Customer

DECIDE to Address the #1 "Leaving Factor" of Clients	
The Leader . . .	The Team. . . .
Encourage a Service-centric environment by demonstrating a willingness to serve, yourself.	Instead of saying, *'It's not my job,'* team members should hear the client's need and, if unable to personally serve the client, that team member should find the right person to meet the need and make the connection.

Customers look to their business providers (of products and services) as the experts in their fields. They need to know that your company is not only equipped but also ready to meet their needs.

DETERMINE that Your Company Holds the Key to a successful outcome	
The Leader . . .	The Team. . . .
Communicate vision and mission.	Tap into professional loyalty and ensure understanding of company vision and mission.
Take care of the *team* to ensure their emotional health.	Communicate needs, in a constructive manner, to leaders.
Empower your team.	Be confident in your ability.

To continue addressing the feeling of indifference for which many clients leave, customers should feel special throughout the service process. Their needs must be addressed as unique.

DESIGN the customer experience	
The Leader . . .	The Team. . . .
Do not have a default approach.	Have a mindset for flexibility.
Design the *complete* customer experience (start to finish).	Understand process and flow of projects.

The follow-through on the company's delivery is vital to the client's perceived feeling of being cared for. It's important that the attention a customer receives is as targeted at the end of the process as it is at the beginning. Most managers and leaders have good intentions and a strong belief that this is the reality of their service:

- 96% of Senior Managers Believe They are Customer-Focused
- 80% of Senior Managers Believe They Deliver "Superior Service"
- ONLY 8% of Customers Believe They RECEIVE "Superior Service"

DELIVER Consistently	
The Leader . . .	The Team. . . .
Maintain communication with clients about their service.	Act on customer feedback without defensiveness.
Communicate important changes as they are adopted.	Be open to change for the sake of client satisfaction and loyalty.

Business is easiest when automated, process-driven, and repeatable. It's the reason why, particularly in trades, manufacturing, and construction, people have been systematically replaced – over the past several decades – with machines and computers. What then makes a company unique more than the people? Even with process-driven delivery, personalization is possible. A CUSTOMIZED customer service is the result, not of the product, but of the team that delivers it. Open-mindedness in approaches and methods may be the difference between a client who feels cared for, and one who is disloyal.

DIFFERENTIATE Through Open-Mindedness	
The Leader . . .	The Team. . . .
Listen to clients.	Seek guidance from leadership to implement customer-communicated needs and goals.
Listen to the team.	Seek support from leadership to deliver customer service to the company-expected level.

You may have noticed a repeating theme that carried over from Team Strengthening to the Improvement of Customer Experience: COMMUNICATION. Leaders need to make communication, positive, encouraging, open-minded, customized communication – a part of everything they do in their company. It is through good communications like those described, that profit can even become a goal through:

Shared, Understood Vision of the Leader

Hardworking, Well-Supported Team Members

Loyal, Satisfied Repeat Customers

The relationships of leader, to team, to clients, to company, all strengthened through communication, are what create the fertile environment for profit.

Record your own UPbeats on the D's of Improved Customer Experience

The test of a first-rate intelligence is the ability to hold two opposed ideas in the mind at the same time, and still retain the ability to function.

~F. Scott Fitzgerald

E is for "Engagement"

Why it Matters

According to Gallup, 29% of American employees are engaged, 53% are not engaged and 18% of American employees are actively DISengaged in the work place.

Most employees hire onto a company and immediately feel like they are a part of a new family. They feel a sense of belonging, even though they are seeking to get to know their new job and work environment. Imagine knowing that your employees all came in ready to move up . . . or move down. How would it affect your management and leadership choices?

Most customers, once they've made a decision to work with a company, feel a sense of accomplishment, having made the decision to move forward on a product or service. They are a part of your family, now, ready to work together toward a common goal. Imagine that every client begins with you on a blank slate. They are able to become your cheerleader or your critic based on the experience you provide.

UPbeat!

Every client is able to become your cheerleader or your critic based on the experience you provide.

How would that knowledge affect the team's delivery of the customer experience?

While, in the professional world, just as in our personal lives, there will be circumstances beyond our control, there is a great deal that we can do to affect positive engagement in a transactional relationship.

Through guidance and support, after the ABC's of Team Strength (**A**cknowledge Thyself, **C**reate a Sense of **B**elonging, and Migrate to the **C**ommunication Comfort Zone), as well as the D's of Customer Experience (**D**ecide, **D**etermine, **D**esign, **D**eliver, and **D**iffer), the desired result is **E** . . . *ENGAGEMENT.* When there is engagement for the team, there is engagement from the client and the leader and company are taken care of, making room for profit.

Abraham Maslow, in 1943, presented a theory that, more than seventy years later, is still a foundational belief about human existence. He developed a pyramid representing the "Hierarchy of Needs" for the human condition. At the lowest level of existence, are the physiological needs for food, water, and shelter from the elements. These are mere SURVIVAL needs. Of course, we have other needs, too, stepping up to

UPbeat!

While Maslow's hierarchy refers to human needs in life, our work is a microcosm of our lives. Therefore, in the workplace, a leader's ultimate goal also must be self-actualization for his team and his clients.

safety, then love and belonging, to worth or self-esteem, to – at the top of the pyramid – a greater purpose (SELF-ACTUALIZATION). While Maslow's hierarchy refers to human needs in life, our work is a microcosm of our lives. Therefore, in the work place, a leader's ultimate goal also must be self-actualization for his team and his clients. Professionally, self-actualization looks like engagement. Note the five tiers of Maslow's hierarchy from the bottom of the tier (Survival) to the top of the tier (Self-Actualization) below:

What does Maslow's hierarchy of needs look like in a professional environment?

Survival

Leaders, employees, and clients at the bottom of the pyramid of needs – in *survival* mode – are ACTIVELY DISENGAGED.

Traits of an employee in survival mode:
- Is there for the money and may even watch the numbers suspiciously
- Arrives as late as possible
- Leaves as soon as possible
- Chooses "quick escape" parking spots
- Watches the clock
- Few internal motivators
- Self-focused

Traits of a client who is ACTIVELY DISENGAGED:
- Seeks the lowest price (for the highest value)
- Offers little networking reciprocation
- Has a lack of loyalty

Traits of a leader at the bottom of the pyramid include:
- Clinging to a job title
- Clinging to authority
- Micro-managing
- Close-minded
- Closed-door policy (not transparent)

An actively disengaged leader can bring down his or her team. An actively disengaged team member can bring down other team members and might even speak poorly of the company to clients.

Actively disengaged clients are likely to publically disparage the company. It's not hard to see how survival mode won't actually allow a company to survive for long.

Leaders need to recognize the traits of employees, clients, and even themselves while being actively disengaged. It is the first step in moving back up the pyramid toward mindsets of thriving and profitability.

UPbeat!

Leaders need to recognize the traits of employees, clients, and even themselves while actively disengaged.

Then, to move beyond survival, a leader must:

- Run team-building activities that allow the discovery of the "something bigger" for which the company is meant
- Highlight the connectiveness between different roles and pieces of the company, as well as between the company and its clients and community
- OPEN communications with clients including addressing questions that could make a company vulnerable such as: *Are we an important part of your team? Do you see us as a partner?*
- Create an environment of dependability on one another in which (much like the definition of partnership in which each party incurs liability for losses and the right to share in the profits), you both make it or you both lose

Security

While stability begins to present itself on the second tier of the pyramid, usually as a result of a leader instilling financial confidence in the company, employees, clients, and leaders in *security* mode are still PASSIVELY DISENGAGED.

Traits of an employee in survival mode:
- Call in sick, or have other absence excuses, often
- Still self-focused, but would be interested in overtime (helps the team, but also helps the employee)
- Seeks justification and blame for work losses and negatives

Traits of a client who is PASSIVELY DISENGAGED:
- Still seeks the lowest price, but will be open to communication and negotiation
- Sees the exchange as a transaction rather than a partnership

Traits of a leader on the second tier of the pyramid include:
- Has a better hold of process and profit than a survivalist, but still not people-focused
- The office door may open, but it's a barricaded corner office

A passively disengaged employee may not be flying the "This Place Sucks" banner, but don't be surprised if he or she has a secret lapel pin. He or she may be unhappy, but usually won't drag others down. Passively disengaged clients may be one and done transactions, rather than looking to the company as a long-term relationship. Leaders can feel overwhelmed when passively disengaged, imagining a company of fully engaged interactions, but not seeing a path to it.

Leaders, when recognizing the traits of the security mode in themselves, employees, or clients, need to stop the negative behaviors before beginning new positive behaviors. This action will take away the overwhelming nature of being on the bottom half of the pyramid with a desire to move up.

To move beyond security, a leader must:
- Create a "no complaint" environment in which challenges are shared in combination with solution suggestions
- Define partnership with clients and work to build trust
- Become accessible by team and clients
- Look deeper into the company's people, processes, team roles, and client relationships to develop a detailed assessment of the areas that may need adjusting

Belonging

Most professional relationships, like personal relationships, start at the middle of the pyramid in *belonging* mode. Employees, clients, and leaders want a sense of belonging and want to understand the mission and the company. The belonging level includes people who are ALMOST ENGAGED.

Traits of an employee in belonging mode:
- The shift from self to others begins here
- Introductions to other company areas begin, along with a desire to understand how things work
- Want to make a difference for the company, but may not understand how to do it yet

Traits of a client who is ALMOST ENGAGED:
- Desires a network or community group that includes your company
- Seeks connections outside of professional environments in sports teams, music, forms of entertainment, and family or friend links

UPbeat!

The drawback of the actively engaged level is that anybody could be pulled up...or down.

Traits of a leader in the middle tier of the pyramid include:
- Moves the focus from process to the people who must implement it
- Recognizes team contributions
- Spends less time in the office and more time in the systems that are part of the company

Almost engaged employees are seeking, but not on, an upward path. Clients who are almost engaged desire connection and leaders have become people-focused.

While most companies operate entirely or almost entirely on the belonging tier of Maslow's hierarchy, the drawback of the almost engaged level is that anybody could be pulled up . . . *or* down. This stage needs to be recognized in order to get the momentum moving in the right direction – UP the pyramid!

To move beyond belonging, a leader must:
- Highlight an upward path for employees
- Identify the pros of a long-term *partnership* with clients
- Set personal and professional goals and communicate them, including – when applicable – to the team

Important

The most difficult part of the second from the top tier of the pyramid is the discovery of self-worth, without arrogance. Often, employees, clients, and leaders might mistake an understanding of their values with egotism. In reality, egotism falls on the bottom of the pyramid with self-focus and outward blame. Knowing one's own value actually contributes to the difference between the almost engaged level and the ENGAGED level.

Traits of an employee in important mode:
- Feels compassion
- Recognize the vital role held in the overall company vision
- Is a doer, still seeking to stand out, but not at the expense of others or the company

Traits of a client who is ENGAGED:

- Feels instrumental in the process of their own customer experience
- Sees his or her own experiences as inspiration for affecting change in their other business-to-business relationships
- Recognizes that helping one another will help them

UPbeat!

Engaged employees don't just belong to the team, they contribute to it.

Traits of a leader in the second-from-the-top tier of the pyramid include:

- Contributes to the whole team's efforts
- Is familiar with the companies SWOT (strengths, weaknesses, threats, and opportunities)
- Recognizes the collaborative nature – between leader, team, clients, and community – of success and profit

Engaged employees don't just belong to the team, they contribute to it. Leaders are guiding the team according to the vision and mission and clients are benefitting from the company's confidence in delivery.

Leaders with a team operating mostly at the engaged level are working beyond the level that most companies usually ever achieve, but some simple outward focusing steps can help bring leaders, employees, and clients, even further up the pyramid

To move beyond important, a leader must:
- Demonstrate a willingness to put others first
- Communicates the value of each role on the team as it relates to the big picture
- Ensures proper team placement for best success

Self-Actualization

The top tier of Maslow's pyramid is the result of an overall adopted philosophy of wanting to help other people. Only 15% of people, whether employees, clients, or leaders, reach self-actualization mode to become HIGHLY ENGAGED.

Traits of an employee in self-actualization mode:
- Loves the job and where they work
- Sees advantage in helping others

Traits of a client who is ENGAGED:
- Is a raving fan of your company to other potential clients
- Enjoys the process and the relationship
- Buys as much as possible from you

Traits of a leader in the top tier of the pyramid include:
- Feels (and outwardly shares) hope with others
- When communicating, acclimates to others, rather than having them acclimate to him or her
- Looks to duplicate him- or herself in others, rather than feeling threatened by others

Highly engaged is the goal! A highly engaged employee can bring up the whole team, and even the leader. Clients not only want to share their experience, but they actually seek opportunities to do so. Leaders see their teams as extended family whose human stories are shared and understood.

To maintain self-actualization, a leader must:
- Seek to understand others
- Build trust through open-mindedness and transparency
- Continue the use of assessments to be consistent about trust, compassion, stability, and hope in the light of changing people, environments, and needs
- Maintain his or her own training
- Provide the necessary training to his or her team
- Keeps clients trained and informed on the processes and products that will affect them

In a highly engaged professional model, there is a positive polarity pulling everybody – team, leader, and clients – to the top of the pyramid.

The company is raved about by clients . . .
. . . who have a great customer experience from a team . . .
. . . that is strengthened by the leader . . .
. . . who is fed by the company.

The leader, in this model, needs to be the one to take up his or her role first so that the cycle of engagement can begin. As with communication, that job starts with awareness.

*I've created a graphic representation of a simple summation of **Maslow's Hierarchy of Needs in the Workplace**.* To download your copy, scan the code at the left or find the graphic online at: https://goo.gl/XOxqlO.

There are only three measurements that tell you nearly everything you need to know about your organization's overall performance: employee engagement, customer satisfaction, and cash flow

~Jack Welch

<u>Training for Engagement</u>

A Coach's Perspective

According to the Brevet Group, 55% of the people making their living in sales don't have the right skills to be successful.

A great deal of the lessons for strengthening the team and improving the customer experience revolve around intangible and immeasurable components related to trust, compassion, stability, and hope. However, three of the six tips for leaders to reach the top of the engagement pyramid are related to one single area. One of the primary areas for which a leader is responsible when it comes to achieving and maintaining a highly engaged work environment is training. In addition to one-on-one sessions, group training, and proprietary resources, my blog touches on topics of importance such as this one.

Read about a relevant concern regarding training, as well as how it can become tangible to the team, as well as to the company's bottom line:

<u>*A Discussion Between a CEO and a CFO*</u>

As the day begins to draw to a close, and the sun is beginning to set beyond the horizon, the Chief Executive Officer (CEO) and Chief Financial Officer

(CFO) are about to cross paths in the hallway. The CFO always has money on his mind as his world is based upon one simple fact: whether or not the actions that he is about to do will cost the company money or make them money.

The CEO, however, comes from a different perspective. He is more interested in whether his next action will improve his team or hurt his team.

The topic of the day for the two individuals includes whether or not to train the sales staff. *'Sure, they could use some training,'* the CFO thought to himself, *'but that will cost the company money.'* He recalls the statistics that he was reminded of earlier:

- 41% of employees at companies with inadequate training programs plan to leave within a year
- 12% of employees at companies that provide excellent training and professional development programs stay at companies past the first year

'Hmmm,' he thought to himself, *'that is pretty compelling especially since the cost of replacing a skilled employee ranges from $75,000 to more than $400,000!'*

The CFO remembers what the consultant told him earlier in the day:

"Companies in the top 25% of training expenditure per employee per year ($1,500 or more) average 24% higher profit margins than

UPbeat!

Companies in the top 25% of training expenditure per employee per year ($1,500 or more) average 24% higher profit margins than companies that spend less.

companies that spend less."

'We sure could use that additional margin,' he reasoned to himself.

His thoughts took him to the last CFO roundtable in which he was involved. He met someone from Motorola and got into an interesting side discussion with him. His eyes widened as he recalled the return on investment that they talk about at Motorola. Motorola estimates that every one dollar that they spend on training yields $29.00 in profit.

'But what about my measurable return on investment (ROI),' he asked himself, already knowing the answer.

Three things will happen:
1. There will be additional revenue generated
2. Productivity/performance improvement will occur
3. Cost reduction is guaranteed

'But this is the way we have always done things,' he justified to himself. *'We are fine,'* he concluded as the CEO approached him.

Needing a quick way to diffuse the argument that was about to erupt, the CFO barked at the CEO: "What happens if we train them and they leave us?" A smile slid across his face as he rested his case, saving the best argument against the cost of training as his opener with the CEO.

The CFO reasoned to the CEO that they would invest this money in the sales team, and then the team would leave and cost the company significant money.

As he was basking in his temporary glory, the CEO quickly replied back to him: "What happens if we don't train them and they stay?"

After the day passed, the chief financial officer determines to learn more about why sales training is a good thing; he jumps in his car and heads home for the evening. He has an uneventful dinner, and then moves into his office to wrap his brain around the internal resistance he always has to sales training. As he is accustomed to doing, he makes his "con" list of some of the reasons that he is opposed to paying for sales training:

1. It is costly
2. It is time-consuming
3. It is not permanent
4. It is better to just add more sales professionals

His mind goes blank. As he stares at the list for what seems like an hour, he reasons with himself that these four reasons are convincing enough. His fingers start to type before he can move away from the computer. Remembering the Motorola example, he decides to start his "pro" sales training list. He finds a staggering statistic on the internet. He stares heavy at his screen. A sigh comes from deep within as he faces the fact: Motorola invests about seven percent of payroll in training. He stops there and quickly does the math in his head.

Was that knot in his stomach from the dollar figure dancing in his head, or from the dinner he doesn't even remember eating? Seven percent of payroll invested in training keeps bouncing in his mind like the neighbor kids' baseball hitting the garage door.

'*Motorola must have a pretty darn good reason to invest that much money,*' he thinks to himself. He refocuses his attention on the computer screen and starts the sentence again that he was reading.

"*Motorola, which invests about seven percent of payroll in training, has averaged a twenty percent productivity improvement over the last four years, compared with a two to five percent improvement for its competitors.*"

'*If someone offered to trade me a $20.00 bill for $7.00, would I would I take it?*' he asked himself. His trusted calculator is at his side. Within minutes, he is hitting the keys on the adding machine faster and more deliberately than usual. He is waiting to see the investment return should his company have similar results to Motorola. Then, with the same anticipation as a grand finale on the Independence Day, came the number staring back at him. It seems to be daring him to prove the formula wrong. He calculates the number again, just to make sure that it is correct; it is!

The home phone rings and it jolts him in his seat, causing him to leave his dreams for a moment and get back to thoughts of the family. "Who could that be," he wonders as he gets up from his chair to focus on a new task.

It was the CEO.

Together they share ideas about sales training, but determine to find more detailed research. After all, if they want the kind of numbers that are still glaring on the calculator readout, there must be some sort of trick to the sales training.

After the call, he continues research and uncovers four different groups of people referring to sales training.

1. **Random** – The company provides no training. Every sales professional does his or her own thing

2. **Informal** – The company provides skills training and encourages sales professionals to apply what they've learned, but they don't monitor or measure the training

3. **Formal** – The company provides skills training and reinforces the use of those skills; it regularly reviews its training processes and adjusts them accordingly

4. **Dynamic** – The company monitors sales professionals' applications of skills and provides continuous feedback, proactively modifying the training process when market conditions change

As he collects his thoughts on his next layer of research, he admitted that his team fell into the first group, as do most in corporate America. He picks up his pen and continued to write the results of these groups and the ROI of the four different categories. While there is some increase at each level, the significant difference he notices is:

- 54 percent of the salespeople in Random companies meet their quotas
- 72 percent of the salespeople receiving Dynamic training meet their quotas

The calculator again heats. He wonders what would happen if an additional ten percent of his team actually meets their sales quota. The numbers stare back at him again. He is now leaning more towards the possibility that sales training would be beneficial to not only the sales team, but also to the company as a whole.

His thoughts turn to the sales management team. "How will they react to this additional work required to see the increase in sales?" he asked himself. He writes down twelve percent on a piece of paper and thinks about dropping this on each of the sales managers' desks, with a note that says, "see me."

He envisions sitting with each of them separately and watching their reactions. If they are open and excited about the idea of seeing their sales increase, then he knows that they are long-term partners to the team. If, however, they are not open and make excuses about how this will not work, he recognizes that they might not be on the same page as the company.

As he sips his coffee and realizes how late it is, he sits back and has a new appreciation for the CEO. He is more committed than ever to listen to those around him and not be close-minded. Already he feels better as he turns off the light in his office.

Record your own UPbeats on E.ngagement!

Part 3:

The Profit Will Come

Excellence is an art won by training and habituation. We do not act rightly because we have virtue or excellence, but we rather have those because we have acted rightly. We are what we repeatedly do. Excellence, then, is not an act but a habit.

~Aristotle

__Guidance and Support__

The Rotating Stage of Successful Leadership

According to the Robert E. Greenleaf Center for Servant Leadership, 65% of employees would take a new leader over a pay raise.

P articularly in the trades, but honestly across the spectrum of careers, the early years of most industries were marked with tyrannical "leaderes" who had fat checks while their employees couldn't afford to eat. Thankfully, those days are past. In the most recent twenty-five years, servant-based leadership has become the new common catchphrase across many professional industries. This "new approach" has come to mean everything from providing expensive ergonomic office spaces with luxuries including health food bars, gyms, and nap areas, to role swap days when leaders take a back seat to plans and ideas that are implemented by entry-level staff, to upside down pay models that have CEOs and executives taking home less than minimum wage while employees without accountability have guaranteed salaries.

Nobody wants to go back to the days of the "Fat Cats," but is this extremist version of "serving" one's employees the right answer? It's true; the leader should care for his or her employees (who then care for the customers, who then care for the company, that then cares for the leader). It's true; the leader should have a servant-based company in that there is a greater purpose . . . a vision . . . to what is being done. It's also true, though, that a team should be able to look to the leaderes, executives, and owners to LEAD, and leading isn't about gimmicks, abdicating responsibilities, or financial martyrdom.

The idea of servant-based leadership is a noble one with positive intentions. However, its meaning has often been misconstrued to the point of leaders forgetting how to actually *lead*. Instead, what if leadership was looked at – not as an upside-down structure with the leader carrying it on his or her shoulders, but as a rotating stage of cycles in which the leader's role changes according to the needs of the team, clients, and company.

Early on in my leadership, my thought was to dictate and review. Dictating was all about telling people what to do, in the case of employees, and telling people what they could expect, in the case of clients. This was a time of step-by-step instruction. Review was a time for me to tell an employee whether or not he or she had achieved the desired result and tell a client how we had fulfilled the expectation. In the "dictate and review" model, the key word was: TELL. There was no cycle. Leaders instructed and others followed (because they had to).

The "Dictate and Review" process was mindless, powerless, and purposeless.

We lost a lot of people. I lost a lot of people. I was threatened by people. On the one hand, I wanted to hire the best of the best who would be able to do the job "as well as me," but – on the other hand – I want them one notch under me. We constantly tried to outdo one another. There's not a lot of learning that happens in that kind of environment. There's no growth because I'd have to be reliant on asking somebody else who I didn't want to know as much as I did. I couldn't get mad at people for what I didn't explain to them. Employees hit a ceiling . . . and so did I.

As I matured in business, so did my model. If I wanted to grow on purpose, I needed to move beyond the days of being a "leader" without going to a misunderstood extreme of the trendy servant-based leadership. It was the cycle I needed to change. Rather than dictate and review, I needed to define the true role of a leader. The new model that I would implement, and that saw my companies through purposeful growth, was built on a cycle of GUIDANCE and SUPPORT.

Guidance because it is the job of the leader to:

- Put purpose, meaning, and vision to every piece of every project so that the team can see how it fits into the bigger picture
- Provide structure and processes to implement the steps of a delivery experience
- Bring network, knowledge, and experience to a company

Support because, it is the job of a leader to:

- Provide the trusting, compassionate, stable, hopeful environment in which to create engaged team and clients
- Communicate with team and clients for clarity and understanding as needed
- Develop the delivery design methods with consideration for all of the operational people, resources, and numbers that come into play

Whether strengthening the team, improving the customer experience, or working with the resulting engagement, the leader takes, not the weight of the world, but the center of the stage. He or she must move fluidly between the roles of guidance, when the team or client needs direction, and support when the team or client needs readjustments and flexibility.

Guidance is different from dictating. In dictating, the step-by-step, micromanaged instructions are given. In guidance, the desired result is communicated and an open-minded discussion takes place to discover the best method for achieving the result. The leader can make decisions based on a combination of team and client input, as well as the knowledge and experience he or she brings.

Support is different from review. In review, there is a simple yes or no as to whether or not something has been achieved. In support, there are frequent check-ins, transparency, and continued communications as the leader offers his or her resources (including finances, but also time, intellect, and expertise) to help the team or the client reach a positive result.

Unlike dictate and review, the guidance and support model is open-minded, empowering, and purpose-driven.

A single end-goal may have multiple guidance sessions and multiple support sessions; the stage is constantly rotating.

Business is often referred to as a game of cards in which everybody is hiding his or her hand. An honest game would have all cards on the table. The reality, though, is that the cards in the professional world are always changing. Business is more of a chess game. If one of the players – the client or the company – makes an unexpected move, there are a number of choices for a next move. The guidance and support model allows for adjustments.

My goal, when I'm speaking, when I'm leading, or when I'm serving a client, is that I want the people listening to leave better than they came. My whole thought process hinges on that goal, achieved through guidance and support.

I want to tell as many people as I can about the ABC's of Team Strength, encouraging people to A.cknowledge their own personality and communication styles, create a sense of B.elonging in their professional worlds, and migrate to one another's C.ommunication comfort zones.

I want people to master the D's of Improving the Customer Experience (D.ecide, D.etermine, D.esign, D.eliver, and D.iffer).

I want people to experience the results of the E (E.ngagement) in their teams, amongst their clients, and in their companies' bottom lines.

I want leaders to implement all of these vital steps through the rotating stage of successful leadership built on guidance and support.

Through these lessons, every business can be . . . *GROWING ON PURPOSE.*

Record your own UPbeats on Guidance and Support

What is your PURPOSEFUL Takeaway?

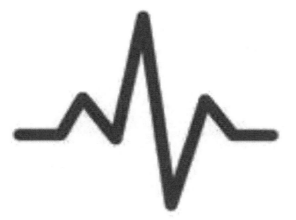

<u>Resources Consulted</u>

As I've noted and credited throughout this book, the insights gained to inspire the learnings shared, have come through a number of respectable polling and surveying organizations. For your convenience, here is a listing of the resources consulted:

- *American Express Survey*
- *American Psychological Association Study on Stress*
- *American Society for Training and Development*
- *Annual Edelman Trust Barometer*
- *Center for American Progress*
- *CPP Global Human Capitol Report*
- *CSO Insights, 2015 Sales Compensation and Performance Management Study*
- *Gallup Poll on Employee Engagement*
- *Gartner, CRM Summit*
- *Gollin/Harris Poll*
- *Groene Consulting*
- *Lee Resources*
- *National Association of Retail Marketing Services*
- *National Study of Manufacturer-Distributor Working Relationships by the Industrial Performance Group, 2002*
- *The American Institute of Stress*
- *Workplace 2000 Employee Insight Survey*

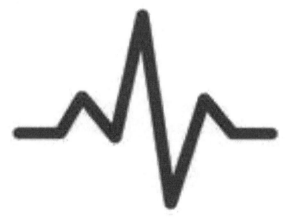

Acknowledgments

I would like to express my gratitude to the many people who saw me through my first book; to all those who provided support, talked things over, read, wrote, offered comments, allowed me to quote their remarks and assisted in the editing, proofreading and design.

I would like to thank Reji Laberje for enabling me to write this book. Without her, I never could have done it! Also, a special thanks to L.J. Hyland, as he introduced me to Reji and totally gave me the confidence that I could do this project.

I would like to thank Michael and Angela Nicloy, for helping me in the process of selection and editing. You guys were a great source of encouragement and energy!

I also want to make sure and thank all my clients and colleagues that have shared their experiences with me so that I could tell others how to "Grow On Purpose"!

In addition, I want to thank K. Paige Engle, for her coaching after the book was done. It is one thing to write a book, it is another thing to get people to read it! Thanks for your expertise!

Above all I want to thank my wife, Kerry and the rest of my family, who supported and encouraged me despite all the time it took me away from them. It was a long journey for them, but very enriching!

Last and not least: I beg forgiveness of all those who have been with me over the course of the years and whose names I have failed to mention.

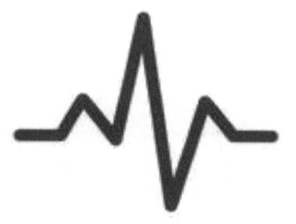

About Your Authors

Dave Molenda
Positive Polarity

Dave Molenda spent twenty years in construction, manufacturing, and manufacturing sales, including ten years building a multi-million dollar company, from scratch, with a focus on commercial and residential windows. In the last years with his company, before selling it for a profit, Molenda began, not just to grow his own company, but help build those of the clients he served. He believed in an abundance mentality . . . that if he helped others to be profitable, so, too, would his own company be profitable! His efforts to meet the needs of his customers led him to learn about communication styles, customization, and a servant's mentality in business. It made the transition to a coaching role an easy choice. With a strong belief in the importance of training, Dave extended his knowledge by becoming certified in DISC and other respectable analysis tools. Today, under his company, "Positive Polarity", he coaches, consults, trains, and presents in the greater Milwaukee area, as well as nationally to manufacturing and architectural professionals, in order to help companies become stronger, internally and externally. In addition to his career with Positive Polarity, Dave is a husband and father who is active in volunteerism and his church community.

*Working with Dave on **"Growing on Purpose"** was **Reji Laberje**, Owner and Creative Director of Reji Laberje Writing and Publishing, where they work toward a better world through better words. Reji is a Bestselling Author with nineteen years of professional-level experience in the*  *writing industry and her fortieth book is hitting the presses in 2016. She lives outside of Milwaukee with her husband of twenty years, Joe, and their active family of seven people and four pets.*

Reji Laberje

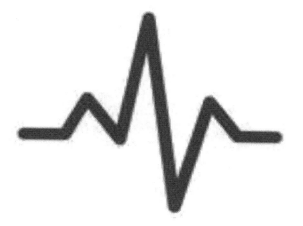

Made in the USA
San Bernardino, CA
13 January 2017